W9-BMF-369

THE SICKNESS UNTO DEATH

KIERKEGAARD'S WRITINGS, XIX

THE SICKNESS UNTO DEATH

A CHRISTIAN PSYCHOLOGICAL
EXPOSITION FOR UPBUILDING
AND AWAKENING

by Søren Kierkegaard

*Edited and Translated
with Introduction and Notes by*

Howard V. Hong and
Edna H. Hong

PRINCETON UNIVERSITY PRESS
PRINCETON, NEW JERSEY

Copyright © 1980 by Howard V. Hong
Published by Princeton University Press, Princeton, New Jersey
In the United Kingdom: Princeton University Press, Chichester, West Sussex

All Rights Reserved

ISBN 0-691-07247-7
ISBN 0-691-02028-0 pbk.

Editorial preparation of this work has been assisted by a
grant from Lutheran Brotherhood, a fraternal benefit society,
with headquarters in Minneapolis, Minnesota

Princeton University Press books are printed on acid-free paper
and meet the guidelines for permanence and durability of the
Committee on Production Guidelines for Book Longevity of the
Council on Library Resources

Designed by Frank Mahood

Printed in the United States of America

First Princeton Paperback printing, with corrections, 1983

14   15   16   17   18   19   20

http://pup.princeton.edu

ISBN-13: 978-0-691-02028-0 (pbk.)

CONTENTS

A. THE SIN OF DESPAIRING OVER ONE'S SIN
109

B. THE SIN OF DESPAIRING OF THE FORGIVENESS OF SINS (OFFENSE)
113

C. THE SIN OF DISMISSING CHRISTIANITY *modo ponendo* [POSITIVELY], OF DECLARING IT TO BE UNTRUTH
125

Early in 1849, a few months before the publication of *The Sickness unto Death* (July 30, 1849), Kierkegaard gave his own estimate that the pseudonymous works by Anti-Climacus (*The Sickness unto Death* and *Practice in Christianity*) are "extremely valuable."[1]

The writing of *The Sickness unto Death* was done in an amazingly short time, mainly during the period March–May 1848. The variations between the final draft and the provisional draft and between the printing manuscript and the final draft are very few, although some changes were of great importance to Kierkegaard himself.

The speed of the writing and the facility with which the manuscript took final form are owing no doubt to Kierkegaard's longstanding concern with the nature and meaning of anxiety and despair in relation to the becoming of the self, questions that were occupying him even more than a decade before the writing of *The Sickness unto Death*. In the Gilleleje letter of 1835 (when Kierkegaard was twenty-two years old), he wrote that a person must "first learn to know himself before learning anything else (γνωθι σεαυτον)."[2] In 1836 he wrote that "the present age is the age of despair."[3] Despair and forgiveness are the theme of a journal entry from 1837,[4] as is also the case in some entries from 1838, one of which includes a reference to Lazarus and the sickness unto death.[5] In the preface to his first book, *From the Papers of One Still Living*, Kierkegaard makes a distinction between what he later calls the "first" and the "deeper self,"[6] and, in his criticism of the substance of Hans Christian Andersen's *Only a Fiddler* as in-

---

[1] *JP* VI 6361 (*Pap.* X¹ A 147).   [2] *JP* V 5100 (*Pap.* I A 75).
[3] *JP* I 737 (*Pap.* I A 181).   [4] *JP* III 3994 (*Pap.* II A 63).
[5] *JP* IV 4001–2 (*Pap.* II A 310).
[6] *KW* I (*SV* XIII 46). See *Four Upbuilding Discourses* (1844), in *Eighteen Upbuilding Discourses, KW* V (*SV* V 94–99).

choate estheticism dependent upon external conditions, he invokes the category of despair without, however, employing the term. Reading what medieval thinkers said about aridity and melancholy (*acedia* and *tristitia*) prompted recollection of "what my father called: A *quiet despair*."[7] Shortly thereafter (July 5, 1840), in considering Kant's and Hegel's emphasis upon mind and theory of knowledge, he made reference to "genuine anthropological contemplation, which has not yet been undertaken."[8] Kierkegaard's entire authorship may in a sense be regarded as the result of his having undertaken that task, and *The Sickness unto Death* is the consummation of his "anthropological contemplation," with despair as a central clue to his anthropology.

All the above-mentioned strains of thought are crystallized in a few lines of a student sermon given on January 12, 1841—lines that could serve as part of the table of contents of *The Sickness unto Death*:

> Or was there not a time also in your consciousness, my listener, when cheerfully and without a care you were glad with the glad, when you wept with those who wept, when the thought of God blended irrelevantly with your other conceptions, blended with your happiness but did not sanctify it, blended with your grief but did not comfort it? And later was there not a time when this in some sense guiltless life, which never called itself to account, vanished? Did there not come a time when your mind was unfruitful and sterile, your will incapable of all good, your emotions cold and weak, when hope was dead in your breast, and recollection painfully clutched at a few solitary memories of happiness and soon these also became loathsome, when everything was of no consequence to you, and the secular bases of comfort found their way to your soul only to wound even more your troubled mind, which impatiently and bitterly turned away from them? Was there not a time when you found no one to whom you could turn, when the

---

[7] *JP* I 739-40 (*Pap.* II A 484-85). See also *JP* I 745 (*Pap.* V A 33).
[8] *JP* I 37 (*Pap.* III A 3).

darkness of quiet despair brooded over your soul, and you did not have the courage to let it go but would rather hang onto it and you even brooded once more over your despair? When heaven was shut for you, and the prayer died on your lips, or it became a shriek of anxiety that demanded an accounting from heaven, and yet you sometimes found within you a longing, an intimation to which you might ascribe meaning, but this was soon crushed by the thought that you were a nothing and your soul lost in infinite space? Was there not a time when you felt that the world did not understand your grief, could not heal it, could not give you any peace, that this had to be in heaven, if heaven was anywhere to be found; alas, it seemed to you that the distance between heaven and earth was infinite, and just as you yourself lost yourself in contemplating the immeasurable world, just so God had forgotten you and did not care about you? And in spite of all this, was there not a defiance in you that forbade you to humble yourself under God's mighty hand? Was this not so? And what would you call this condition if you did not call it death, and how would you describe it except as darkness? But then when hope . . ..[9]

If these lines may be regarded as an epitomization of Kierkegaard's anthropological contemplation to that date, *The Concept of Anxiety* (June 17, 1844), by Vigilius Haufniensis, and *The Sickness unto Death* may be regarded as a two-stage explication. Both are based on the concept of man as a synthesis of the finite and the infinite, the temporal and the eternal. Anxiety is the "dizziness of freedom, which emerges when the spirit wants to posit the synthesis, and freedom now looks down into its own possibility, laying hold of finiteness to support itself."[10] *The Sickness unto Death* presupposes anxiety but excludes it from consideration, inasmuch as despair is a more advanced stage: "in all despair there is an interplay of finitude and infinitude, of the divine and the human, of free-

[9] *JP* IV 3915 (*Pap.* III C 1).
[10] *The Concept of Anxiety*, p. 61, *KW* VIII (*SV* IV 331).

dom and necessity."[11] Anxiety is touched upon very briefly in
The Sickness unto Death by way of the analogy of dizziness,[12]
but the exclusion of a consideration of anxiety in the advance
to an analysis of despair is emphasized by the removal of allusions to anxiety and its related concept of hereditary sin.[13] The
relation between anxiety, despair, and sin is signaled, however, in "the dialectic of sin,"[14] because "sin presupposes itself "[15] through anxiety.

The resolution of the dialectic of despair/healed despair is
also foreshadowed in a nonpseudonymous discourse published to accompany *The Concept of Anxiety*: "To Need God
Is a Human Being's Highest Perfection."[16] A condensation
is given in the *Papirer*: "If man did not have absolute need
of God, he could not (1) know himself—self-knowledge,
(2) be immortal."[17] This is reformulated in the very compact
summation in *The Sickness unto Death*: "The formula that describes the state of the self when despair is completely
rooted out is this: in relating itself to itself and in willing to be
itself, the self rests transparently in the power that established
it."[18] In the journals from the period before the publication of
The Sickness unto Death there are entries that develop this
theme,[19] themselves reaching a climax in the profound and
moving entry on forgiveness and becoming spirit,[20] which
was written shortly before Kierkegaard began intensive work
on the manuscript of *The Sickness unto Death*.

In the context of the prolonged concern with the nature and
possible forms of anxiety, sin, and despair, the crystallized
idea of *The Sickness unto Death* first appeared in the journals of
1847. An entry surrounded by datable entries referring to
pericope texts and to newspaper items between April 5 and 26
reads: "At first perhaps a person sins out of weakness, yields
to weakness (alas, for your weakness is the strength of lust,

---

[11] Supplement, p. 145 (*Pap.* VIII² B 168:6).   [12] Pp. 14, 16.
[13] See Supplement, p. 156 (*Pap.*VIII² B 166).   [14] Pp. 101, 120.
[15] P. 89.   [16] See note 6. Ibid. (*SV* V 81–105).
[17] *JP* I 53 (*Pap.* V B 196).   [18] P. 14; see also pp. 49, 131.
[19] See *JP* III 3698; IV 4010, 4594 (*Pap.*VIII¹ A 130, 32, 64).
[20] *JP* 167 (*Pap.* VIII¹ A 673).

inclination, passion, and sin); but then he becomes so despondent over his sin that he perhaps sins again and sins out of despair."[21] This is echoed in subsequent entries,[22] and an entry presumably from February 1848 contains the lines:

A new book ought to be written entitled: *Thoughts that Cure Radically, Christian Healing.* . . . It will have two parts, perhaps it is better to have three.

    (1) First comes: Thoughts that wound from behind[23]— for upbuilding. . . .[24]
        (1) [*changed from:* (2)] On the consciousness of sin,
           The Sickness unto Death
           Christian Discourses
        (2) [*changed from:* (3)] *Radical Cure*
           [*changed from:* Thoughts that Cure Radically]
           Christian Healing
           The Atonement[25]

Given the long incubation period, the idea of *The Sickness unto Death* readily found its form and development. The form is algebraic,[26] along the lines of its earlier counterpart, *The Concept of Anxiety*; and of all the works, this one most clearly and compactly develops a single theme.

In substance, *The Sickness unto Death* (1849) is related to *The Concept of Anxiety* (1844) in the sense that despair is an advanced stage beyond anxiety. *Philosophical Fragments* (1844) is a hypothesis: *If* an advance is to be made upon Socrates, *then* what follows? *Concluding Unscientific Postscript* (1846) presents

---

[21] *JP* IV 4010 (*Pap.* VIII¹ A 64).

[22] See, for example, *JP* IV 4013 (*Pap.* VIII¹ A 497), from around the end of 1847.

[23] Already used as the title of Part Three of *Christian Discourses* (April 26, 1848), *KW* XVII (*SV* X 163).

[24] See note 57 below; Supplement, p. 137 (title page).

[25] *JP* V 6110 (*Pap.* VIII¹ A 558). Part (2) subsequently became *Practice in Christianity*.

[26] "Algebraic" (*algebraisk*) refers to the compact, abstract, dialectical form of works such as *The Concept of Anxiety, Philosophical Fragments,* and *The Sickness unto Death.* See *KW* VII (*SV* IV 254), VIII (IV 382, 395, 403), XIX (XI 194, *Bogstavregning*).

the universally human (the Socratic) and Christianity in a positive ascent. *The Sickness unto Death* presents the Socratic and Christianity in a correlation of complementary discontinuity. *Practice in Christianity* (1850), developed as a separate work, is an expressive, indicative ethic, in contrast to the hidden inwardness of *The Sickness unto Death*.

Having completed the draft of *The Sickness unto Death*, Kierkegaard considered recasting it as a lyrical discourse in a more rhetorical form. In a journal entry from May 13, 1848, with the heading "Report on 'The Sickness unto Death,' " he wrote:

> There is one difficulty with this book: it is too dialectical and stringent for the proper use of the rhetorical, the soul-stirring, the gripping. The title itself seems to indicate that it should be discourses—the title is lyrical.
>
> Perhaps it cannot be used at all, but in any case it is enriched with an excellent plan which always can be used, but less explicitly, in discourses.
>
> The point is that before I really can begin using the rhetorical I always must have the dialectical thoroughly fluent, must have gone through it many times. That was not the case here.[27]

In the margin he added:

> If it is to be structured rhetorically, it must be structured rhetorically under certain main points, each of which would become one discourse. . . . No. 1. Its hiddenness. . . . No. 2. Its universality. . . . No. 3. Its continuance. . . . No. 4. Where is it situated? In the self. . . .
>
> But the point is that the task is much too great for a rhetorical arrangement, since in that case every single individual figure would also have to be depicted poetically. The dialectical algebra [*Bogstavregning*] works better.[28]

Although Kierkegaard gave some further consideration to a possible recasting of the work,[29] he held to his judgment that

---

[27] *JP* V 6136 (*Pap.* VIII¹ A 651).   [28] *JP* V 6137 (*Pap.* VIII¹ A 652).
[29] See *JP* V 6138 (*Pap.* VIII¹ A 653).

"the dialectical algebra works better." Furthermore, in addition to work on what eventually was called *Practice in Christianity*, he became immersed in prolix deliberations about giving up writing, about publishing works at hand, about pseudonymity in writing and publishing, and about a possible appointment to a rural pastorate.

The external occasion of the extended agonizing deliberation was the publication of the second edition of *Either/Or*,[30] which appeared on May 14, 1849. Consideration was given to adding a retraction of the work in the new edition.[31] Although this was not done, Kierkegaard thought that it "will never do to let the second edition of *Either/Or* be published without something accompanying it. Somehow the accent must be that I have made up my mind about being a religious author. . . ."

Furthermore, the other books ("The Sickness unto Death," "Come Here," "Blessed Is He Who Is Not Offended")[32] are extremely valuable. In one of them in particular[33] it was granted to me to illuminate Christianity on a scale greater than I had ever dreamed possible; crucial categories are directly disclosed there. Consequently, it must be published. . . .

But the second edition of *Either/Or* is a critical point (as I did in fact regard it originally and wrote "The Point of View" to be published simultaneously with it and otherwise would scarcely have been in earnest about publishing the second edition)—it will never come again. If this opportunity is not utilized, everything I have written, viewed as a totality, will be dragged down into the esthetic.[34]

"My intention was to publish all the completed manuscripts [*The Sickness unto Death*, parts of *Practice in Christianity*, *The Point of View*, *Armed Neutrality*, *Two Ethical-Religious Essays*] in one volume, all under my name—and then

---

[30] See *Letters*, Letters 152-57, *KW* XXV.
[31] *JP* VI 6374 (*Pap.* X[1] A 192).
[32] The second and third "books" became parts of *Practice in Christianity*.
[33] *Practice in Christianity*.   [34] *JP* VI 6361 (*Pap.* X[1] A 147).

to make a clean break."[35] At the same time, Kierkegaard was giving serious consideration to the possibility of an appointment to a rural pastorate, but finally it became clear to him that it was beyond his ability "to undertake both at once."[36]

At bottom, however, the reflective predicament centered in the complex of issues involved in pseudonymity, in the tension between poetic ideality and personal actuality, in the concept and practice of the "religious poet." On the one hand, Kierkegaard thought that what was needed was "a detachment of poets; almost sinking under the demands of the ideal, with the glow of a certain unhappy love they set forth the ideal. . . . These religious poets must have the particular ability to do the kind of writing which helps people out into the current."[37] On the other hand, the "wrong way is much too close: wanting to reform, to arouse the whole world—instead of oneself, and this certainly is the wrong way for hotheads with a lot of imagination."[38] Kierkegaard did finally come to a decision, but the transmuted poignancy and radicality of this complex of issues appear even in the opening pages of Part Two of *The Sickness unto Death*.[39]

After Kierkegaard had determined "to lay aside everything I had finished writing," he decided again "that it might be unjustifiable for me to let these writings just lie there. . . ."[40] "Perhaps it would be best to publish all the last four books ('The Sickness unto Death,' 'Come to Me,' 'Blessed Is He Who Is Not Offended,' 'Armed Neutrality') in one volume under the title

Collected Works of Consummation

with 'The Sickness unto Death' as Part I."[41]

A little later he widened the sphere, saying that perhaps "all the writings that lie finished (the most valuable I have

---

[35] *JP* VI 6517 (*Pap.* X² A 147).   [36] Ibid.
[37] *JP* VI 6521 (*Pap.* X² A 157).
[38] *JP* VI 6432 (*Pap.* X¹ A 513).   [39] Pp. 77-78.
[40] *JP* VI 6517 (*Pap.* X² A 147), a retrospective entry from November 1849, shortly after the publication of *The Sickness unto Death*.
[41] *JP* VI 6271 (*Pap.* IX A 390).

produced) can also be used, but, for God's sake, in such a way as to guarantee that they are kept poetic as poetic awakening."[42] The penultimate decision with regard to publication, therefore, was to maintain pseudonymity and to restrict the number of works so as to exclude all those with a direct personal reference.

Just as the Guadalquibir River at some place plunges underground and then comes out again, so I must now plunge into pseudonymity, but I also understand now how I will emerge again under my own name. The important thing left is to do something about seeking an appointment and then to travel.

(1) The three small ethical-religious essays will be anonymous; this was the earlier stipulation. (2) "The Sickness unto Death" will be pseudonymous and is to be gone through so that my name and the like are not in it. (3) The three works, "Come Here, All You," "Blessed Is He Who Is Not Offended," and "From on High He Will Draw All to Himself" will be pseudonymous. Either all three in one volume under the common title, "Practice in Christianity, Attempt by————," or each one separately. They are to be checked so that my name and anything about me etc. are excluded, which is the case with number three. (4) Everything under the titles "The Point of View for My Work as an Author," "A Note," "Three Notes," and "Armed Neutrality" cannot conceivably be published.[43]

Despite a residual ambivalence about publishing and although "there is no hurry about publishing," Kierkegaard did speak with publisher Carl A. Reitzel, "who said he dared not take on anything new for publication."[44] This was troublesome to Kierkegaard, because he had been pondering too long over many issues. "Earlier, of course, I had had misgivings," he wrote in a retrospective journal entry, "and they promptly

---

[42] *JP* VI 6337 (*Pap.* X¹ A 95).

[43] *JP* VI 6416 (*Pap.* X¹ A 422), June 4, 1849, three weeks before delivery of the manuscript of *The Sickness unto Death* to the printer.

[44] Ibid.

returned: what should I do with all the writing that now lay completed. If I got an appointment first, then it could hardly be published. . . ." Meanwhile, he tried to see the Minister of Church and Education and Bishop Mynster. He missed the former, and the latter had no free time the day that Kierkegaard called on him.

During the same period I had been reading Fénelon and Tersteegen. Both had made a powerful impact on me. A line by Fénelon struck me especially: that it must be dreadful for a man if God had expected something more from him. Misgivings awakened full force as to whether such a change in my personal life could even take place. On the other hand, I was qualified to be an author, and I still had money. It seemed to me that I had allowed myself to panic too soon and to hope for what I desired but perhaps could not attain and thus perhaps would make a complete mess of things.

So I wrote to the printer. I was informed that their services were available and could they receive the manuscript the next day; decisions are seldom made that fast.[45]

Kierkegaard had already had enough practical problems and issues of principle to preoccupy him almost to the point of immobility apart from writing. Then, the evening before he was to deliver the manuscript, he learned that Regine Olsen's father had died.

That affected me powerfully. Strangely enough, he had died one or two days before I had heard of it, and I learned of it only after my arrangement with the printer. I said to myself: If you had found out about it before you wrote to the printer, you perhaps would have held back in order to see if this could have some significance, however firmly I was convinced that it was extremely dubious to speak to her precisely because I deceived her by pretending I was a deceiver.[46]

[45] *JP* VI 6762 (*Pap*. X⁴ A 299).
[46] Ibid. Concerning an approach to Regine, see *Letters, KW* XXV, Letters 235–39.

Sleeping poorly that night, he imagined that someone spoke to him or that he talked to himself in a nocturnal conversation.

I remember the words: See, now he intends his own destruction. But I cannot say for sure whether it was because it was I who wanted to call off sending the manuscript to the printer and make an overture to her, or the reverse, that it was I who stood firm on sending the manuscript to the printer. I can also remember the words: After all, it is no concern of (but I cannot remember exactly whether the word was *yours* or *mine*) that Councilor Olsen is dead. I can remember the words but not the particular pronoun: You—or I—could, in fact, wait a week. I can remember the reply: Who does he think he is.[47]

There was something terrifying about the nocturnal conversation. It seemed that he was being frightened away from something, something from which he himself wanted to be excused. But at the same time he considered "that God's terrifying a man does not always signify that this is the thing he should refrain from but that it is the very thing he should do, but he has to be shocked in order to learn to do it in fear and trembling."

So I sent the manuscript to the printer. I prayed God to educate me so that in the tension of actuality I might learn how far I should go. I desperately needed a decision; it had been a frightful strain to have those manuscripts lying there and every single day to think of publishing them, while correcting a word here and there.

Then the book [*The Sickness unto Death*] was made pseudonymous. That much was dismissed.[48]

"This was a real education, and it is still by no means finished."[49]

Kierkegaard's self-education in the writing of *The Sickness*

[47] *JP* VI 6762 (*Pap.* X⁴ A 299).
[48] Ibid.
[49] *JP* VI 6820 (*Pap.* X⁴ A 647).

unto Death is reflected in the late changes in the printing manuscript, resulting in the use of Anti-Climacus as the pseudonymous author and the designation of Kierkegaard as the editor.[50] Humbled under the ideality of the work, he could not venture to publish it under his own name. "It is poetry—and therefore my life, to my humiliation, must obviously express the opposite, the inferior."[51]

It is absolutely right—a pseudonym had to be used.

When the demands of ideality are to be presented at their maximum, then one must take extreme care not to be confused with them himself, as if he himself were the ideal.

Protestations could be used to avoid this. But the only sure way is this redoubling.

The difference from the earlier pseudonyms is simply but essentially this, that I do not retract the whole thing humorously[52] but identify myself as one who is striving.[53]

The use of the pseudonym Anti-Climacus not only epitomizes Kierkegaard's decisive termination of more than a year of agonizing self-reflection and deliberation about publishing, but it also marks a turn in the entire authorship. "So I turn off the tap; that means the pseudonym Anti-Climacus, a halt,"[54] he wrote in July, while *The Sickness unto Death* was being printed. The "halt" refers to a qualitative shift in the authorship and to the halt he was brought to under the critique of the writings, not simply to the termination of writing and publishing.

My task was to pose this riddle of awakening: a balanced esthetic and religious productivity, simultaneously.

---

[50] See Supplement, pp. 137, 139 (title page; *Pap.* VIII² B 171:1-5).

[51] *JP* VI 6501 (*Pap.* X² A 66).

[52] The reference is to Johannes Climacus, who at the end of *Concluding Unscientific Postscript* declared that the book was superfluous and that no one should cite it as an authority, because to be an authority is too burdensome for a humorist. Therefore the book has no conclusion, only a revocation. See *KW* XII (*SV* VII 537-43, Appendix).

[53] *JP* VI 6446 (*Pap.* X¹ A 548).

[54] *JP* VI 6450 (*Pap.* X¹ A 557).

This has been done. There is balance even in quantity. *Concluding Postscript* is the midpoint. . . .
What comes next cannot be added impatiently as a conclusion. For dialectically it is precisely right that this be the end.[55]

The dialectical halt is further clarified in an entry from October 1849: "one points to something higher that examines a person critically and forces him back within his boundaries."[56] At the time that *The Sickness unto Death* was published, Kierkegaard stated the levels of the authorship in relation to himself: "there is a stretch that is mine: the upbuilding;[57] behind and ahead lie the lower[58] and the higher pseudonymities;[59] the upbuilding is mine, but not the es-

[55] *JP* VI 6347 (*Pap.* X¹ A 118).

[56] *JP* VI 6518 (*Pap.* X⁵ B 206).

[57] The preface to *Two Upbuilding Discourses* (1843) and the prefaces to the subsequent five volumes of discourses (1843-44) state that the book "is called 'discourses,' not sermons, because its author does not have authority to *preach*, 'upbuilding discourses,' not discourses for upbuilding, because the speaker by no means claims to be a *teacher*." "For upbuilding," Kierkegaard wrote in a journal entry pertaining to *The Sickness unto Death*, "is more than my category, the poet-category: upbuilding" (*JP* VI 6431; *Pap.* X¹ A 510). The "upbuilding" includes, therefore, *Eighteen Upbuilding Discourses* (*KW* V) and other signed discourses: *Three Discourses on Imagined Occasions* (*KW* X), *Upbuilding Discourses in Various Spirits* (*KW* XV), *Works of Love* (*KW* XVI), *Christian Discourses* (*KW* XVII), and *The Lily of the Field and the Bird of the Air* (*KW* XVIII), which refers to the preface to *Two Upbuilding Discourses* (1843) and was published a few weeks before *The Sickness unto Death*. See note 61 below.

[58] The lower pseudonyms are Victor Eremita, Mr. A, Judge William, Johannes de Silentio, Constantin Constantius, Johannes Climacus, Vigilius Haufniensis, Nicolaus Notabene, Hilarius Bookbinder, Frater Taciturnus, and Inter et Inter, the editors or authors of the whole or a part of *Either/Or*, *Fear and Trembling*, *Repetition*, *Fragments* and *Postscript*, *The Concept of Anxiety*, *Prefaces*, *Stages*, and *The Crisis and a Crisis in the Life of an Actress*. Kierkegaard (Kjerkegaard on title page) is stated as the editor of the earliest work, *From the Pages of One Still Living*, but no pseudonym is used.

[59] The higher pseudonyms are H. H., the author of *Two Ethical-Religious Essays* (published May 19, 1849, six weeks before *The Sickness unto Death*) and Anti-Climacus. See note 58 above; Supplement, p. 140 (*Pap.* X¹ A 530); *JP* V 6349, 6462 (*Pap.* X⁶ B 48; X¹ A 594).

thetic,[60] not the pseudonymous works for upbuilding,[61] either, and even less those for awakening."[62]

Obviously the pseudonym Anti-Climacus has a special relation to the pseudonym Johannes Climacus, the author of the early *De omnibus dubitandum est, Philosophical Fragments,* and *Concluding Unscientific Postscript.* The prefix "Anti" may be misleading, however. It does not mean "against." It is an old form of "ante" (before), as in "anticipate," and "before" also denotes a relation of rank, as in "before me" in the First Commandment.

> Johannes Climacus and Anti-Climacus have several things in common; but the difference is that whereas Johannes Climacus places himself so low that he even says that he himself is not a Christian,[63] one seems to be able to detect in Anti-Climacus that he considers himself to be a Christian on an extraordinarily high level . . . I would place myself higher than Johannes Climacus, lower than Anti-Climacus.[64]

[60] Kierkegaard regarded all the works by the lower pseudonyms (see note 58 above) as esthetic. In the preface to *The Lily of the Field and the Bird of the Air* (published at the same time as the second edition of *Either/Or,* May 14, 1849), Kierkegaard stated that "it is offered with the right hand," in contrast to the pseudonymous work, "which was held out and is held out with the left" (*KW* XVIII; *SV* X 15). The same differentiating observation pertains to all the esthetic works or lower pseudonymous works and to the upbuilding works (see note 57 above).

[61] Included among the pseudonymous works "for upbuilding" are presumably *Two Ethical-Religious Essays,* by H. H., and the Anti-Climacus works *Practice in Christianity* and *The Sickness unto Death* (with "for Upbuilding" on the title page). The phrase is used on the division page of Part Three of the signed work *Upbuilding Discourses in Various Spirits.* See *JP* VI 6431, 6436, 6438 (*Pap.* X¹ A 510, 520, 529).

[62] *JP* VI 6461 (*Pap.* X¹ A 593). In a sense, the entire authorship was "for awakening" through the positing of a choice between the esthetical and the religious (see *JP* VI 6520; *Pap.* X² A 150). However, the expression "for awakening" is used for the pseudonymous works by Anti-Climacus: *The Sickness unto Death* (see title page) and *Practice in Christianity* (see p. 5). In *The Point of View,* Kierkegaard used the expression "epigram of awakening" (*KW* XXII; *SV* XIII 557). See *JP* VI 6436, 6438 (*Pap.* X¹ A 520, 529).

[63] *Postscript, KW* XII (*SV* VII 537, 539).

[64] *JP* VI 6433 (*Pap.* X¹ A 517). See *Letters, KW* XXV, Letter 213 (July 1849).

The shift to Anti-Climacus as author and to Kierkegaard as editor was made to preclude any confusion of Kierkegaard himself with the ideality of the book. As a further precaution, Kierkegaard contemplated an "Editor's Note" at the end and wrote a number of drafts.[65] None was used, for a number of reasons: possible misinterpretation, the presence in *The Sickness unto Death* of references to the religious poet (which allude to Kierkegaard himself), a deeper understanding of the new pseudonym, and a contradiction of such a note by a portion of *Practice in Christianity* on making observations.[66]

In December 1848, some months after the basic writing of *The Sickness unto Death* and six months before the decision to print it, Kierkegaard sketched a plan and even wrote an introduction[67] for "a few discourses dealing with the most beautiful and noble, humanly speaking, forms of despair. . . ."[68] Although one of the themes came to be developed in *Practice in Christianity*,[69] the plan was never actualized. If it had been fulfilled, it would have been the counterpart of *The Sickness unto Death*.

[65] See Supplement, pp. 157-61 (*Pap.* X⁵ B 15, 16, 18-20).
[66] *KW* XX (*SV* XII 213-17).
[67] See Supplement, pp. 163-65 (*Pap.* IX A 498-500).
[68] See Supplement, p. 163 (*Pap.* IX A 421).
[69] *KW* XX (*SV* XII 137 ff.).

THE SICKNESS UNTO DEATH

*A CHRISTIAN PSYCHOLOGICAL
EXPOSITION FOR UPBUILDING
AND AWAKENING*

by Anti-Climacus

Herr! gieb uns blöde Augen
für Dinge, die nichts taugen,
und Augen voller Klarheit
in alle deine Wahrheit.

[Lord, give us weak eyes
for things of little worth,
and eyes clear-sighted
in all of your truth.]

Many may find the form of this "exposition" strange; it may seem to them too rigorous to be upbuilding and too upbuilding to be rigorously scholarly. As far as the latter is concerned, I have no opinion. As to the former, I beg to differ; if it were true that it is too rigorous to be upbuilding, I would consider it a fault. It is, of course, one thing if it cannot be upbuilding for everyone, because not everyone is qualified to do its bidding; that it has the character of the upbuilding is something else again. From the Christian point of view, everything, indeed everything, ought to serve for upbuilding.[1] The kind of scholarliness and scienticity that ultimately does not build up is precisely thereby unchristian. Everything essentially Christian must have in its presentation a resemblance to the way a physician speaks at the sickbed; even if only medical experts understand it, it must never be forgotten that the situation is the bedside of a sick person. It is precisely Christianity's relation to life (in contrast to a scholarly distance[2] from life) or the ethical aspect of Christianity that is upbuilding, and the mode of presentation, however rigorous it may be otherwise, is completely different, qualitatively different, from the kind of scienticity and scholarliness that is "indifferent," whose lofty heroism is so far, Christianly, from being heroism that, Christianly, it is a kind of inhuman curiosity. It is Christian heroism—a rarity, to be sure—to venture wholly to become oneself, an individual human being, this specific individual human being, alone before God, alone in this prodigious strenuousness and this prodigious responsibility; but it is not Christian heroism to be taken in by the idea of man in the abstract or to play the wonder game with world history.[3] All Christian knowing, however rigorous its form, ought to be concerned, but this concern is precisely the upbuilding. Concern constitutes the relation to life, to the actuality of the personality, and therefore earnestness from the Christian point of view; the loftiness of indifferent knowledge is, from the Christian point of view, a long way from being more earnest—Christianly, it is a witticism, an affectation. Earnestness, on the other hand, is the upbuilding.

Therefore, in one sense this little book is such that a college student could write it, in another sense, perhaps such that not every professor could write it.

But that the form of the treatise is what it is[4] has at least been considered carefully, and seems to be psychologically correct as well. There is a more formal style that is so formal that it is not very significant and, once it is all too familiar, readily becomes meaningless.

Just one more comment, no doubt unnecessary, but nevertheless I will make it: once and for all may I point out that in the whole book, as the title indeed declares, despair is interpreted as a sickness, not as a cure. Despair is indeed that dialectical. Thus, also in Christian terminology death is indeed the expression for the state of deepest spiritual wretchedness, and yet the cure is simply to die, to die to the world.[5]

1848

"This sickness is not unto death" (John 11:4). And yet
Lazarus did die; when the disciples misunderstood what
Christ added later, "Our friend Lazarus has fallen asleep, but I
go to awaken him out of sleep" (11:11), he told them flatly
"Lazarus is dead" (11:14).[6] So Lazarus is dead, and yet this
sickness was not unto death; he was dead, and yet this sickness is not unto death. We know that Christ had in mind the
miracle that would permit his contemporaries, "if they would
believe, to see the glory of God" (11:40), the miracle by which
He raised Lazarus from the dead; therefore "this sickness"
was not only not unto death, but, as Christ predicted, was
"for the glory of God, so that the Son of God may be glorified
by means of it" (11:4). But even if Christ did not resurrect
Lazarus, is it not still true that his sickness, death itself, is not
unto death? When Christ approaches the grave and cries out
with a loud voice, "Lazarus, come out" (11:43), is it not plain
that "this" sickness is not unto death? But even if Christ had
not said that, does not the mere fact that He who is "the resur-
rection and the life" (11:25) approaches the grave signify that
this sickness is not unto death: the fact that Christ exists, does
it not mean that *this* sickness is not unto death! What good
would it have been to Lazarus to be resurrected from the dead
if ultimately he had to die anyway—of what good would it
have been to Lazarus if He were not He who is the resurrec-
tion and the life for everyone who believes in Him! No, it
may be said that *this* sickness is not unto death, not because
Lazarus was raised from the dead, but because He exists;
therefore this sickness is not unto death. Humanly speaking,
death is the last of all, and, humanly speaking, there is hope
only as long as there is life. Christianly understood, however,
death is by no means the last of all; in fact, it is only a minor
event within that which is all, an eternal life, and, Christianly

understood, there is infinitely much more hope in death than there is in life—not only when in the merely human sense there is life but this life in consummate health and vitality.

Christianly understood, then, not even death is "the sickness unto death"; even less so is everything that goes under the name of earthly and temporal suffering: need, illness, misery, hardship, adversities, torments, mental sufferings, cares, grief. And even if such things were so hard and painful that we human beings or at least the sufferer, would declare, "This is worse than death"—all those things, which, although not sickness, can be compared with a sickness, are still, Christianly understood, not the sickness unto death.

That is how sublimely Christianity has taught the Christian to think about earthly and worldly matters, death included. It is almost as if the Christian might become haughty because of this proud elevation over everything that men usually call misfortune or the worst of evils. Nevertheless, Christianity has in turn discovered a miserable condition that man as such does not know exists. This miserable condition is the sickness unto death. What the natural man catalogs as appalling—after he has recounted everything and has nothing more to mention—this to the Christian is like a jest. Such is the relation between the natural man and the Christian; it is like the relation between a child and an adult: what makes the child shudder and shrink, the adult regards as nothing. The child does not know what the horrifying is; the adult knows and shrinks from it. The child's imperfection is, first, not to recognize the horrifying, and then, implicit in this, to shrink from what is not horrifying. So it is also with the natural man: he is ignorant of what is truly horrifying, yet is not thereby liberated from shuddering and shrinking—no, he shrinks from that which is not horrifying. It is similar to the pagan's relationship to God: he does not recognize the true God, but to make matters worse, he worships an idol as God.

Only the Christian knows what is meant by the sickness unto death. As a Christian, he gained a courage that the natural man does not know, and he gained this courage by learning to fear something even more horrifying. This is the way a person always gains courage; when he fears a greater danger, he always has the courage to face a lesser one; when he is exceedingly afraid of one danger, it is as if the others did not exist at all. But the most appalling danger that the Christian has learned to know is "the sickness unto death."

Part One

THE SICKNESS UNTO DEATH
IS DESPAIR

A

Despair Is the Sickness
unto Death[1]

A.
DESPAIR IS A SICKNESS OF THE SPIRIT, OF THE SELF, AND ACCORDINGLY CAN TAKE THREE FORMS: IN DESPAIR NOT TO BE CONSCIOUS OF HAVING A SELF (NOT DESPAIR IN THE STRICT SENSE); IN DESPAIR NOT TO WILL TO BE ONESELF; IN DESPAIR TO WILL TO BE ONESELF

A human being is spirit. But what is spirit? Spirit is the self. But what is the self? The self is a relation that relates itself to itself or is the relation's relating itself to itself in the relation; the self is not the relation but is the relation's relating itself to itself. A human being is a synthesis of the infinite and the finite, of the temporal and the eternal, of freedom and necessity, in short, a synthesis.[2] A synthesis is a relation between two. Considered in this way, a human being is still not a self.

In the relation between two, the relation is the third as a negative unity,[3] and the two relate to the relation and in the relation to the relation; thus under the qualification of the psychical the relation between the psychical and the physical is a relation. If, however, the relation relates itself to itself, this relation is the positive third, and this is the self.[4]

Such a relation that relates itself to itself, a self, must either have established itself or have been established by another.

If the relation that relates itself to itself has been established by another, then the relation is indeed the third, but this relation, the third, is yet again a relation and relates itself to that which established the entire relation.

The human self is such a derived, established relation, a relation that relates itself to itself and in relating itself to itself relates itself to another. This is why there can be two forms of despair in the strict sense. If a human self had itself established itself, then there could be only one form: not to will to be oneself, to will to do away with oneself, but there could not be the form: in despair to will to be oneself. This second formulation is specifically the expression for the complete dependence of the relation (of the self), the expression for the inability of the self to arrive at or to be in equilibrium and rest by itself, but only, in relating itself to itself, by relating itself to that which has established the entire relation. Yes, this second form of despair (in despair to will to be oneself) is so far from designating merely a distinctive kind of despair that, on the contrary, all despair ultimately can be traced back to and be resolved in it. If the despairing person is aware of his despair, as he thinks he is, and does not speak meaninglessly of it as of something that is happening to him (somewhat as one suffering from dizziness[5] speaks in nervous delusion of a weight on his head or of something that has fallen down on him, etc., a weight and a pressure that nevertheless are not something external but a reverse reflection of the internal) and now with all his power seeks to break the despair by himself and by himself alone—he is still in despair and with all his presumed effort only works himself all the deeper into deeper despair. The misrelation of despair is not a simple misrelation but a misrelation in a relation that relates itself to itself and has been established by another, so that the misrelation in that relation which is for itself [*for sig*][6] also reflects itself infinitely in the relation to the power that established it.

The formula that describes the state of the self when despair is completely rooted out is this: in relating itself to itself and in willing to be itself, the self rests transparently in the power that established it.

XI
129

B.

THE POSSIBILITY AND THE ACTUALITY OF DESPAIR[7]

Is despair an excellence or a defect? Purely dialectically, it is both. If only the abstract idea of despair is considered, without any thought of someone in despair, it must be regarded as a surpassing excellence. The possibility of this sickness is man's superiority over the animal, and this superiority distinguishes him in quite another way than does his erect walk, for it indicates infinite erectness or sublimity, that he is spirit.[8] The possibility of this sickness is man's superiority over the animal; to be aware of this sickness is the Christian's superiority over the natural man; to be cured of this sickness is the Christian's blessedness.

Consequently, to be able to despair is an infinite advantage, and yet to be in despair is not only the worst misfortune and misery—no, it is ruination. Generally this is not the case with the relation between possibility and actuality.[9] If it is an excellence to be able to be this or that, then it is an even greater excellence to be that; in other words, to be is like an ascent when compared with being able to be. With respect to despair, however, to be is like a descent when compared with being able to be; the descent is as infinitely low as the excellence of possibility is high. Consequently, in relation to despair, not to be in despair is the ascending scale. But here again this category is equivocal. Not to be in despair is not the same as not being lame, blind, etc. If not being in despair signifies neither more nor less than not being in despair, then it means precisely to be in despair. Not to be in despair must signify the destroyed possibility of being able to be in despair; if a person is truly not to be in despair, he must at every moment destroy the possibility. This is generally not the case in the relation between actuality and possibility. Admittedly, thinkers say that actuality is annihilated possibility, but that is not entirely true; it is the consummated, the active possibility.[10] Here, on the contrary, the actuality (not to be in despair) is the impotent, destroyed possibility, which is why it is also a negation; although actuality in relation to possibility is usually a corroboration, here it is a denial.

XI
130

Despair is the misrelation in the relation of a synthesis that relates itself to itself.[11] But the synthesis is not the misrelation; it is merely the possibility, or in the synthesis lies the possibility of the misrelation.[12] If the synthesis were the misrelation, then despair would not exist at all, then despair would be something that lies in human nature as such. That is, it would not be despair; it would be something that happens to a man, something he suffers, like a disease to which he succumbs, or like death, which is everyone's fate. No, no, despairing lies in man himself. If he were not a synthesis, [13]he could not despair at all; nor could he despair if the synthesis in its original state from the hand of God were not in the proper relationship.

[14]Where, then, does the despair come from? From the relation in which the synthesis relates itself to itself, inasmuch as God, who constituted man a relation, releases it from his hand, as it were—that is, inasmuch as the relation relates itself to itself. And because the relation is spirit, is the self, upon it rests the responsibility for all despair at every moment of its existence, however much the despairing person speaks of his despair as a misfortune and however ingeniously he deceives himself and others, confusing it with that previously mentioned case of dizziness, with which despair, although qualitatively different, has much in common, since dizziness[15] corresponds, in the category of the psychical, to what despair is in the category of the spirit, and it lends itself to numerous analogies to despair.

Once the misrelation, despair, has come about, does it continue as a matter of course? No, it does not continue as a matter of course; if the misrelation continues, it is not attributable to the misrelation but to the relation that relates itself to itself. That is, every time the misrelation manifests itself and every moment it exists, it must be traced back to the relation. For example, we say that someone catches a sickness, perhaps through carelessness. The sickness sets in and from then on is in force and is an *actuality* whose origin recedes more and more into the *past*. It would be both cruel and inhuman to go on saying, "You, the sick person, are in the process of catching the sickness right now." That would be the same as perpetually wanting to dissolve the actuality of the sickness into its possibility. It is true that he was responsible for catching the sickness, but he did that only once; the continuation of the sickness is a simple result of his catching it that one time, and its progress cannot be traced at every moment to him as the cause; he brought it upon himself, but it cannot be said that he *is bringing* it upon himself. To despair, however, is a different matter. Every actual moment of despair is traceable to possibility; every moment he is in despair he *is bringing* it upon himself. It is always the present tense; in relation to the actuality there is no pastness of the past: in every actual moment of despair the person in despair bears all the past as a present in possibility. The reason for this is that to despair is a qualification of spirit and relates to the eternal in man. But he cannot rid himself of the eternal—no, never in all eternity. He cannot throw it away once and for all, nothing is more impossible; at any moment that he does not have it, he must have thrown it or is throwing it away—but it comes again, that is, every moment he is in despair he is bringing his despair upon himself. For despair is not attributable to the misrelation but to the relation that relates itself to itself. A person cannot rid himself of the relation to himself any more than he can rid himself of his self, which, after all, is one and the same thing, since the self is the relation to oneself.[16]

C.[17]
DESPAIR IS "THE SICKNESS UNTO DEATH"

XI
131

This concept, the sickness unto death, must, however, be understood in a particular way. Literally it means a sickness of which the end and the result are death. Therefore we use the expression "fatal sickness" as synonymous with the sickness unto death. In that sense, despair cannot be called the sickness unto death. Christianly understood, death itself is a passing into life. Thus, from a Christian point of view, no earthly, physical sickness is the sickness unto death, for death is indeed the end of the sickness, but death is not the end. If there is to be any question of a sickness unto death in the strictest sense, it must be a sickness of which the end is death and death is the end. This is precisely what despair is.

But in another sense despair is even more definitely the sickness unto death. Literally speaking, there is not the slightest possibility that anyone will die from this sickness or that it will end in physical death. On the contrary, the torment of despair is precisely this inability to die. Thus it has more in common with the situation of a mortally ill person when he lies struggling with death and yet cannot die. Thus to be sick *unto* death is to be unable to die, yet not as if there were hope of life; no, the hopelessness is that there is not even the ultimate hope, death. When death is the greatest danger, we hope for life; but when we learn to know the even greater danger, we hope for death. When the danger is so great that death becomes the hope, then despair is the hopelessness of not even being able to die.

It is in this last sense that despair is the sickness unto death, this tormenting contradiction, this sickness of the self, perpetually to be dying, to die and yet not die, to die death. For to die signifies that it is all over, but to die death means to experience dying, and if this is experienced for one single moment, one thereby experiences it forever. If a person were to die of despair as one dies of a sickness, then the eternal in him, the self, must be able to die in the same sense as the body dies of sickness. But this is impossible; the dying of despair continually converts itself into a living. The person in despair cannot die; "no more than the dagger can slaughter thoughts"[18] can despair consume the eternal, the self at the root of despair, whose worm does not die and whose fire is not quenched.[19] Nevertheless, despair is veritably a self-consuming, but an impotent self-consuming that cannot do what it wants to do. What it wants to do is to consume itself, something it cannot do, and this impotence is a new form of self-consuming, in which despair is once again unable to do what it wants to do, to consume itself; this is an intensification, or the law of intensification. This is the provocativeness or the cold fire in despair, this gnawing that burrows deeper and deeper in impotent self-consuming. The inability of despair to consume him is so remote from being any kind of comfort to the person in despair that it is the very opposite. This comfort is precisely the torment, is precisely what keeps the gnawing alive and keeps life in the gnawing, for it is precisely over this that he despairs (not as having despaired): that he cannot consume himself, cannot get rid of himself, cannot reduce himself to nothing. This is the formula for despair raised to a higher power, the rising fever in this sickness of the self.

An individual in despair despairs over *something*. So it seems for a moment, but only for a moment; in the same moment the true despair or despair in its true form shows itself. In despairing over *something*, he really despaired over *himself*, and now he wants to be rid of himself. For example, when the ambitious man whose slogan is "Either Caesar or nothing"[20] does not get to be Caesar, he despairs over it. But this also means something else: precisely because he did not get to be Caesar, he now cannot bear to be himself. Consequently he does not despair because he did not get to be Caesar but despairs over himself because he did not get to be Caesar. This self, which, if it had become Caesar, would have been in seventh heaven (a state, incidentally, that in another sense is just as despairing), this self is now utterly intolerable to him. In a deeper sense, it is not his failure to become Caesar that is intolerable, but it is this self that did not become Caesar that is intolerable; or, to put it even more accurately, what is intolerable to him is that he cannot get rid of himself. If he had become Caesar, he would despairingly get rid of himself, but he did not become Caesar and cannot despairingly get rid of himself. Essentially, he is just as despairing, for he does not have his self, is not himself. He would not have become himself by becoming Caesar but would have been rid of himself, and by not becoming Caesar he despairs over not being able to get rid of himself. Thus it is superficial for someone (who probably has never seen anyone in despair, not even himself) to say of a person in despair: He is consuming himself. But this is precisely what he in his despair [wants] and this is precisely what he to his torment cannot do, since the despair has inflamed something that cannot burn or be burned up in the self.

Consequently, to despair over something is still not despair proper. It is the beginning, or, as the physician says of an illness, it has not yet declared itself. The next is declared despair,

XI
133

to despair over oneself. A young girl despairs of love, that is, she despairs over the loss of her beloved, over his death or his unfaithfulness to her. This is not declared despair; no, she despairs over herself. This self of hers, which she would have been rid of or would have lost in the most blissful manner had it become "his" beloved, this self becomes a torment to her if it has to be a self without "him." This self, which would have become her treasure (although, in another sense, it would have been just as despairing), has now become to her an abominable void since "he" died, or it has become to her a nauseating reminder that she has been deceived. Just try it, say to such a girl, "You are consuming yourself," and you will hear her answer, "Oh, but the torment is simply that I cannot do that."

<sub xi>XI
134</sub> [21]To despair over oneself, in despair to will to be rid of oneself—this is the formula for all despair. Therefore the other form of despair, in despair to will to be oneself, can be traced back to the first, in despair not to will to be oneself, just as we previously resolved the form, in despair not to will to be oneself, into the form, in despair to will to be oneself (see A). A person in despair despairingly wills to be himself. But if he despairingly wills to be himself, he certainly does not want to be rid of himself. Well, so it seems, but upon closer examination it is clear that the contradiction is the same. The self that he despairingly wants to be is a self that he is not (for to will to be the self that he is in truth is the very opposite of despair), that is, he wants to tear his self away from the power that established it. In spite of all his despair, however, he cannot manage to do it; in spite of all his despairing efforts, that power is the stronger and forces him to be the self he does not want to be. But this is his way of willing to get rid of himself, to rid himself of the self that he is in order to be the self that he has dreamed up. He would be in seventh heaven to be the self he wants to be (although in another sense he would be just as despairing), but to be forced to be the self he does not want to be, that is his torment—that he cannot get rid of himself.

Socrates demonstrated the immortality of the soul from the fact that sickness of the soul (sin) does not consume it as sickness of the body consumes the body.[22] Thus, the eternal in a person can be demonstrated by the fact that despair cannot consume his self, that precisely this is the torment of contradiction in despair. If there were nothing eternal in a man, he could not despair at all; if despair could consume his self, then there would be no despair at all.

Such is the nature of despair, this sickness of the self, this sickness unto death. The despairing person is mortally ill. In a completely different sense than is the case with any illness, this sickness has attacked the most vital organs, and yet he cannot die. Death is not the end of the sickness, but death is incessantly the end. To be saved from this sickness by death is an impossibility, because the sickness and its torment—and the death—are precisely this inability to die.

This is the state in despair. No matter how much the despairing person avoids it, no matter how successfully he has completely lost himself (especially the case in the form of despair that is ignorance of being in despair) and lost himself in such a manner that the loss is not at all detectable—eternity nevertheless will make it manifest that his condition was despair and will nail him to himself so that his torment will still be that he cannot rid himself of his self, and it will become obvious that he was just imagining that he had succeeded in doing so. Eternity is obliged to do this, because to have a self, to be a self, is the greatest concession, an infinite concession, given to man, but it is also eternity's claim upon him.

XI
135

B

The Universality of This Sickness (Despair)

Just as a physician might say that there very likely is not one single living human being who is completely healthy, so anyone who really knows mankind might say that there is not one single living human being who does not despair a little, who does not secretly harbor an unrest, an inner strife, a disharmony, an anxiety about an unknown something or a something he does not even dare to try to know, an anxiety about some possibility in existence or an anxiety about himself, so that, just as the physician speaks of going around with an illness in the body, he walks around with a sickness, carries around a sickness of the spirit that signals its presence at rare intervals in and through an anxiety he cannot explain. In any case, no human being ever lived and no one lives outside of Christendom who has not despaired, and no one in Christendom if he is not a true Christian, and insofar as he is not wholly that, he still is to some extent in despair.

No doubt this observation will strike many people as a paradox, an overstatement, and also a somber and depressing point of view. But it is none of these things. It is not somber, for, on the contrary, it tries to shed light on what generally is left somewhat obscure; it is not depressing but instead is elevating, inasmuch as it views every human being under the destiny of the highest claim upon him, to be spirit; nor is it a paradox but, on the contrary, a consistently developed basic view, and therefore neither is it an overstatement.

However, the customary view of despair does not go beyond appearances, and thus it is a superficial view, that is, no view at all. It assumes that every man must himself know best whether he is in despair or not. Anyone who says he is in despair is regarded as being in despair, and anyone who thinks he is not is therefore regarded as not. As a result, the phenomenon of despair is infrequent rather than quite common. That one is in despair is not a rarity; no, it is rare, very rare, that one is in truth not in despair.

The common view has a very poor understanding of despair. Among other things, it completely overlooks (to name only this, which, properly understood, places thousands and thousands and millions in the category of despair), it completely overlooks that not being in despair, not being conscious of being in despair, is precisely a form of despair. In a much deeper sense, the position of the common view in interpreting despair is like that of the common view in determining whether a person is sick—in a much deeper sense, for the common view understands far less well what spirit is (and lacking this understanding, one cannot understand despair, either) than it understands sickness and health. As a rule, a person is considered to be healthy when he himself does not say that he is sick, not to mention when he himself says that he is well. But the physician has a different view of sickness. Why? Because the physician has a defined and developed conception of what it is to be healthy and ascertains a man's condition accordingly. The physician knows that just as there is merely imaginary sickness there is also merely imaginary health, and in the latter case he first takes measures to disclose the sickness. Generally speaking, the physician, precisely because he is a physician (well informed), does not have complete confidence in what a person says about his condition. If everyone's statement about his condition, that he is healthy or sick, were completely reliable, to be a physician would be a delusion. A physician's task is not only to prescribe remedies but also, first and foremost, to identify the sickness, and consequently his first task is to ascertain whether the supposedly sick person is actually sick or whether the supposedly healthy person is perhaps actually sick. Such is also the relation of the physician of the soul to despair. He knows what despair is; he recognizes it and therefore is satisfied neither with a person's declaration that he is not in despair nor with his declaration that he is. It must be pointed out that in a certain sense it is not even always the case that those who say they despair are in despair. Despair can be affected, and as a qualification of the spirit it may also be mistaken for and confused with all sorts of transitory states, such as dejection, inner conflict, which pass without developing into despair. But the physician of the soul properly regards these also as forms of despair; he sees very well that they are affectation. Yet this very affectation is despair: he sees very well that this dejection etc. are not of great significance, but precisely this—that it has and acquires no great significance—is despair.

The common view also overlooks that despair is dialectically different from what is usually termed a sickness, because it is a sickness of the spirit. Properly understood, this dialectic again brings thousands under the definition of despair. If at a given time a physician has made sure that someone is well, and that person later becomes ill, then the physician may legitimately say that this person at one time was healthy but now is sick. Not so with despair. As soon as despair becomes apparent, it is manifest that the individual was in despair. Hence, at no moment is it possible to decide anything about a person who has not been saved by having been in despair, for whenever that which triggers his despair occurs, it is immediately apparent that he has been in despair his whole life. On the other hand, when someone gets a fever, it can by no means be said that it is now apparent that he has had a fever all his life. Despair is a qualification of the spirit, is related to the eternal, and thus has something of the eternal in its dialectic.

Despair is not only dialectically different from a sickness, but all its symptoms are also dialectical, and therefore the superficial view is very easily deceived in determining whether or not despair is present. Not to be in despair can in fact signify precisely to be in despair, and it can signify having been rescued from being in despair. A sense of security and tranquillity can signify being in despair; precisely this sense of security and tranquillity can be the despair, and yet it can signify having conquered despair and having won peace. Not being in despair is not similar to not being sick, for not being sick cannot be the same as being sick, whereas not being in despair can be the very same as being in despair. It is not with despair as with a sickness, where feeling indisposed is the sickness. By no means. Here again the indisposition is dialectical. Never to have sensed this indisposition is precisely to be in despair.

This means and has its basis in the fact that the condition of man, regarded as spirit (and if there is to be any question of despair, man must be regarded as defined by spirit), is always critical. We speak of a crisis in relation to sickness but not in relation to health. Why not? Because physical health is an immediate qualification that first becomes dialectical in the condition of sickness, in which the question of a crisis arises. Spiritually, or when man is regarded as spirit, both health and sickness are critical; there is no immediate health of the spirit.

As soon as man ceases to be regarded as defined by spirit (and in that case there can be no mention of despair, either) but only as psychical-physical synthesis, health is an immediate qualification, and mental or physical sickness is the only dialectical qualification.[23] But to be unaware of being defined as spirit is precisely what despair is. Even that which, humanly speaking, is utterly beautiful and lovable—a womanly youthfulness that is perfect peace and harmony and joy—is nevertheless despair. To be sure, it is happiness, but happiness is not a qualification of spirit, and deep, deep within the most secret hiding place of happiness there dwells also anxiety, which is despair; it very much wishes to be allowed to remain there, because for despair the most cherished and desirable place to live is in the heart of happiness. Despite its illusory security and tranquillity, all immediacy is anxiety and thus, quite consistently, is most anxious about nothing. The most gruesome description of something most terrible does not make immediacy as anxious as a subtle, almost carelessly, and yet deliberately and calculatingly dropped allusion to some indefinite something—in fact, immediacy is made most anxious by a subtle implication that it knows very well what is being talked about. Immediacy probably does not know it, but reflection never snares so unfailingly as when it fashions its snare out of nothing, and reflection is never so much itself as when it is—nothing. It requires extraordinary reflection, or, more correctly, it requires great faith to be able to endure reflection upon nothing—that is, infinite reflection. Consequently, even that which is utterly beautiful and lovable, womanly youthfulness, is still despair, is happiness. For that reason, it is impossible to slip through life on this immediacy. And if this happiness does succeed in slipping through, well, it is of little use, for it is despair. Precisely because the sickness of despair is totally dialectical, it is the worst misfortune never to have had that sickness: it is a true godsend to get it, even if it is the most dangerous of illnesses, if one does not want to be cured of it. Generally it is regarded as fortunate to be cured of a sickness; the sickness itself is the misfortune.

XI
140

Therefore, [24]the common view that despair is a rarity is entirely wrong; on the contrary, it is universal. The common view, which assumes that everyone who does not think or feel he is in despair is not or that only he who says he is in despair is, is totally false. On the contrary, the person who without affectation says that he is in despair is still a little closer, is dialectically closer, to being cured than all those who are not regarded as such and who do not regard themselves as being in despair. The physician of souls will certainly agree with me that, on the whole, most men live without ever becoming conscious of being destined as spirit[25]—hence all the so-called security, contentment with life, etc., which is simply despair. On the other hand, those who say they are in despair are usually either those who have so deep a nature that they are bound to become conscious as spirit or those whom bitter experiences and dreadful decisions have assisted in becoming conscious as spirit: it is either the one or the other; the person who is really devoid of despair is very rare indeed.

There is so much talk about human distress and wretchedness—I try to understand it and have also had some intimate acquaintance with it—there is so much talk about wasting a life, but only that person's life was wasted who went on living so deceived by life's joys or its sorrows that he never became decisively and eternally conscious as spirit, as self, or, what amounts to the same thing, never became aware and in the deepest sense never gained the impression that there is a God and that "he," he himself, his self, exists before this God—an infinite benefaction that is never gained except through despair. What wretchedness that so many go on living this way, cheated of this most blessed of thoughts! What wretchedness that we are engrossed in or encourage the human throng to be engrossed in everything else, using them to supply the energy for the drama of life but never reminding them of this blessedness. What wretchedness that they are lumped together and deceived instead of being split apart so that each individual may gain the highest, the only thing worth living for and enough to live in for an eternity. I think that I could weep an eternity over the existence of such wretchedness! And to me an even more horrible expression of this most terrible sickness and misery is that it is hidden—not only that the person suffering from it may wish to hide it and may succeed, not only that it can so live in a man that no one, no one detects it, no, but also that it can be so hidden in a man that he himself is not aware of it! And when the hourglass has run out, the hourglass of temporality, when the noise of secular life has grown silent and its restless or ineffectual activism has come to an end, when everything around you is still, as it is in eternity, then—whether you were man or woman, rich or poor, dependent or independent, fortunate or unfortunate, whether you ranked with royalty and wore a glittering crown or in humble obscurity bore the toil and heat of the day, whether your name will be remembered as long as the world stands and consequently as long as it stood or you are nameless and run nameless in the innumerable multitude, whether the magnificence encompassing you surpassed all human description or the most severe and ignominious human judgment befell you—eternity asks you and every individual in these millions and millions about only one thing: whether you have lived in despair or not, whether you have despaired in such a way that you did not realize that you were in despair, or in such a way that you covertly carried this sickness inside of you as your gnawing secret, as a fruit of sinful love under your heart, or in such a way that you, a terror to others, raged

XI
141

in despair. And if so, if you have lived in despair, then, regardless of whatever else you won or lost, everything is lost for you, eternity does not acknowledge you, it never knew you—or, still more terrible, it knows you as you are known and it binds you to yourself in despair.

C

The Forms of This Sickness (Despair)

The forms of despair may be arrived at abstractly by reflecting upon the constituents of which the self as a synthesis is composed. The self is composed of infinitude and finitude. However, this synthesis is a relation, and a relation that, even though it is derived, relates itself to itself, which is freedom.[26] The self is freedom. But freedom is the dialectical aspect of the categories of possibility and necessity.

However, despair must be considered primarily within the category of consciousness; whether despair is conscious or not constitutes the qualitative distinction between despair and despair. Granted, all despair regarded in terms of the concept is conscious, but this does not mean that the person who, according to the concept, may appropriately be said to be in despair is conscious of it himself. Thus, consciousness is decisive. Generally speaking, consciousness—that is, self-consciousness—is decisive with regard to the self. The more consciousness, the more self; the more consciousness, the more will; the more will, the more self. A person who has no will at all is not a self; but the more will he has, the more self-consciousness he has also.

A.

DESPAIR CONSIDERED WITHOUT REGARD TO ITS BEING CONSCIOUS OR NOT, CONSEQUENTLY ONLY WITH REGARD TO THE CONSTITUENTS OF THE SYNTHESIS

a. *Despair as Defined by Finitude/Infinitude*

The self is the conscious synthesis of infinitude and finitude that relates itself to itself, whose task is to become itself, which can be done only through the relationship to God. To become oneself is to become concrete. But to become concrete is neither to become finite nor to become infinite, for that which is to become concrete is indeed a synthesis. Consequently, the progress of the becoming must be an infinite moving away from itself in the infinitizing of the self, and an infinite coming back to itself in the finitizing process. But if the self does not become itself, it is in despair, whether it knows that or not. Yet every moment that a self exists, it is in a process of becoming, for the self κατὰ δύναμιν [in potentiality] does not actually exist, is simply that which ought to come into existence. Insofar, then, as the self does not become itself, it is not itself; but not to be itself is precisely despair.

α. *Infinitude's Despair Is to Lack Finitude*

That this is so is due to the dialectic inherent in the self as a synthesis, and therefore each constituent is its opposite. No form of despair can be defined directly (that is, undialectically), but only by reflecting upon its opposite. The condition of the person in despair can be described directly, as the poet in fact does by giving him lines to speak.[27] But the despair can be defined only by way of its opposite, and if the lines are to have any poetic value, the coloring of the expression must contain the reflection of the dialectical opposite. Consequently, every human existence that presumably has become or simply wants to be infinite, in fact, every moment in which
a human existence has become or simply wants to be infinite, is despair. For the self is the synthesis of which the finite is the limiting and the infinite the extending constituent. Infinitude's despair, therefore, is the fantastic, the unlimited, for the self is healthy and free from despair only when, precisely by having despaired, it rests transparently in God.

The fantastic, of course, is most closely related to the imagination [*Phantasie*], but the imagination in turn is related to feeling, knowing, and willing; therefore a person can have imaginary feeling, knowing, and willing. As a rule, imagination is the medium for the process of infinitizing; it is not a capacity, as are the others—if one wishes to speak in those terms, it is the capacity *instar omnium* [for all capacities]. When all is said and done, whatever of feeling, knowing, and willing a person has depends upon what imagination he has, upon how that person reflects himself—that is, upon imagination. Imagination is infinitizing reflection, and therefore the elder Fichte[28] quite correctly assumed that even in relation to knowledge the categories derive from the imagination. The self is reflection, and the imagination is reflection, is the rendition of the self as the self's possibility. The imagination is the possibility of any and all reflection, and the intensity of this medium is the possibility of the intensity of the self.

The fantastic is generally that which leads a person out into the infinite in such a way that it only leads him away from himself and thereby prevents him from coming back to himself.

When feeling becomes fantastic in this way, the self becomes only more and more volatilized and finally comes to be a kind of abstract sentimentality that inhumanly belongs to no human being but inhumanly combines sentimentally, as it were, with some abstract fate—for example, humanity *in abstracto.* Just as the rheumatic is not master of his physical sensations, which are so subject to the wind and weather that he involuntarily detects any change in the weather etc., so also the person whose feeling has become fantastic is in a way infinitized, but not in such a manner that he becomes more and more himself, for he loses himself more and more.

So also with knowing, when it becomes fantastic. The law for the development of the self with respect to knowing, insofar as it is the case that the self becomes itself, is that the increase of knowledge corresponds to the increase of self-knowledge, that the more the self knows, the more it knows itself. If this does not happen, the more knowledge increases, the more it becomes a kind of inhuman knowledge, in the obtaining of which a person's self is squandered, much the way men were squandered on building pyramids, or the way men in Russian brass bands are squandered on playing just one note, no more, no less.[29]

The self is likewise gradually volatilized when willing be-

XI
145

comes fantastic. Willing, then, does not continually become proportionately as concrete as it is abstract, so that the more infinite it becomes in purpose and determination, the more personally present and contemporary it becomes in the small part of the task that can be carried out at once, so that in being infinitized it comes back to itself in the most rigorous sense,[30] so that when furthest away from itself (when it is most infinite in purpose and determination), it is simultaneously and personally closest to carrying out the infinitely small part of the work that can be accomplished this very day, this very hour, this very moment.

When feeling or knowing or willing has become fantastic, the entire self can eventually become that, whether in the more active form of plunging headlong into fantasy or in the more passive form of being carried away, but in both cases the person is responsible. The self, then, leads a fantasized existence in abstract infinitizing or in abstract isolation, continually lacking its self, from which it only moves further and further away. Take the religious sphere, for example. The God-relationship is an infinitizing, but in fantasy this infinitizing can so sweep a man off his feet that his state is simply an intoxication. To exist before God may seem unendurable to a man because he cannot come back to himself, become himself. Such a fantasized religious person would say (to characterize him by means of some lines): "That a sparrow can live is comprehensible; it does not know that it exists before God. But to know that one exists before God, and then not instantly go mad or sink into nothingness!"

XI
146

But to become fantastic in this way, and thus to be in despair, does not mean, although it usually becomes apparent, that a person cannot go on living fairly well, seem to be a man, be occupied with temporal matters, marry, have children, be honored and esteemed—and it may not be detected that in a deeper sense he lacks a self. Such things do not create much of a stir in the world, for a self is the last thing the world cares about and the most dangerous thing of all for a person to show signs of having. The greatest hazard of all, losing the self, can occur very quietly in the world, as if it were nothing at all. No other loss can occur so quietly; any other loss—an arm, a leg, five dollars, a wife, etc.—is sure to be noticed.

β. *Finitude's Despair Is to Lack Infinitude*

That this is so is due, as pointed out under α, to the dialectic inherent in the self as a synthesis, and therefore each constituent is its opposite.

To lack infinitude is despairing reductionism, narrowness. Of course, what is meant here is only ethical narrowness and limitation. As a matter of fact, in the world there is interest only in intellectual or esthetic limitation or in the indifferent (in which there is the greatest interest in the world), for the secular mentality is nothing more or less than the attribution of infinite worth to the indifferent. The secular view always clings tightly to the difference between man and man and naturally does not have any understanding of the one thing needful[31] (for to have it is spirituality), and thus has no understanding of the reductionism and narrowness involved in having lost oneself, not by being volatilized in the infinite, but by being completely finitized, by becoming a number instead of a self, just one more man, just one more repetition of this everlasting *Einerlei* [one and the same].

Despairing narrowness is to lack primitivity or to have robbed oneself of one's primitivity, to have emasculated oneself in a spiritual sense. Every human being is primitively intended to be a self, destined to become himself, and as such every self certainly is angular, but that only means that it is to be ground into shape, not that it is to be ground down smooth, not that it is utterly to abandon being itself out of fear of men, or even simply out of fear of men not to dare to be itself in its more essential contingency (which definitely is not to be ground down smooth), in which a person is still himself for himself. But whereas one kind of despair plunges wildly into the infinite and loses itself, another kind of despair seems to permit itself to be tricked out of its self by "the others." Surrounded by hordes of men, absorbed in all sorts of secular matters, more and more shrewd about the ways of the world—such a person forgets himself, forgets his name divinely understood, does not dare to believe in himself, finds it too hazardous to be himself and far easier and safer to be like the others, to become a copy, a number, a mass man.

Now this form of despair goes practically unnoticed in the world. Just by losing himself this way, such a man has gained an increasing capacity for going along superbly in business and social life, indeed, for making a great success in the world. Here there is no delay, no difficulty with his self and its infinitizing; he is as smooth as a rolling stone, as *courant* [passable] as a circulating coin. He is so far from being regarded as a person in despair that he is just what a human being is supposed to be. As is natural, the world generally has no understanding of what is truly appalling. The despair that not only does not cause one any inconvenience in life but makes life cozy and comfortable is in no way, of course, regarded as despair. That this is the world's view is borne out, for example, by practically all the proverbs, which are nothing more than rules of prudence. For example, we say that one regrets ten times for having spoken to once for having kept silent—and why? Because the external fact of having spoken can involve one in difficulties, since it is an actuality. But to have kept silent! And yet this is the most dangerous of all. For by maintaining silence, a person is thrown wholly upon himself; here actuality does not come to his aid by punishing him, by heaping the consequences of his speaking upon him. No, in this respect it is easy to keep silent. But the person who knows what is genuinely appalling fears most of all any mistake, any sin that takes an inward turn and leaves no outward trace. The world considers it dangerous to venture in this way—and why? Because it is possible to lose. Not to venture is prudent. And yet, precisely by not venturing it is so terribly easy to lose what would be hard to lose, however much one lost by risking, and in any case never this way, so easily, so completely, as if it were nothing at all—namely, oneself. If I have ventured wrongly, well, then life helps me by punishing mc. But if I have not ventured at all, who helps me then? Moreover, what if by not venturing at all in the highest sense (and to venture in the highest sense is precisely to become aware of oneself) I cowardly gain all earthly advantages—and lose myself![32]

So it is with finitude's despair. Because a man is in this kind of despair, he can very well live on in temporality, indeed, actually all the better, can appear to be a man, be publicly acclaimed, honored, and esteemed, be absorbed in all the temporal goals. [33]In fact, what is called the secular mentality consists simply of such men who, so to speak, mortgage themselves to the world. They use their capacities, amass money, carry on secular enterprises, calculate shrewdly, etc., perhaps make a name in history, but themselves they are not; spiritually speaking, they have no self, no self for whose sake they could venture everything, no self before God—however self-seeking they are otherwise.

b. *Despair as Defined by Possibility/Necessity*

XI
148

Possibility and necessity are equally essential to becoming (and the self has the task of becoming itself in freedom). Possibility and necessity belong to the self just as do infinitude and finitude (ἄπειρον/πέρας [the unlimited/limited]).[34] A self that has no possibility is in despair, and likewise a self that has no necessity.

α. *Possibility's Despair Is to Lack Necessity*

XI
148

That this is so is due, as pointed out previously, to the dialectic [inherent in the self as a synthesis].

Just as finitude is the limiting aspect in relation to infinitude, so also necessity is the constraint in relation to possibility. Inasmuch as the self as a synthesis of finitude and infinitude is established, is κατὰ δύναμιν [potential], in order to become itself it reflects itself in the medium of imagination, and thereby the infinite possibility becomes manifest. The self is κατὰ δύναμιν [potentially] just as possible as it is necessary, for it is indeed itself, but it has the task of becoming itself. Insofar as it is itself, it is the necessary, and insofar as it has the task of becoming itself, it is a possibility.

But if possibility outruns necessity so that the self runs

XI
149

away from itself in possibility, it has no necessity to which it is to return; this is possibility's despair. This self becomes an abstract possibility; it flounders in possibility until exhausted but neither moves from the place where it is nor arrives anywhere, for necessity is literally that place; to become oneself is literally a movement in that place. To become is a movement away from that place, but to become oneself is a movement in that place.

Thus possibility seems greater and greater to the self; more and more it becomes possible because nothing becomes actual. Eventually everything seems possible, but this is exactly the point at which the abyss swallows up the self. It takes time for each little possibility to become actuality. Eventually, however, the time that should be used for actuality grows shorter and shorter; everything becomes more and more momentary. Possibility becomes more and more intensive—but in the sense of possibility, not in the sense of actuality, for the intensive in the sense of actuality means to actualize some of what is possible. The instant something appears to be possible, a new possibility appears, and finally these phantasmagoria follow one another in such rapid succession that it seems as if everything were possible, and this is exactly the final moment, the point at which the individual himself becomes a mirage.

What the self now lacks is indeed actuality, and in ordinary language, too, we say that an individual has become unreal. However, closer scrutiny reveals that what he actually lacks is necessity. The philosophers are mistaken when they explain necessity as a unity of possibility and actuality—no, actuality is the unity of possibility and necessity.[35] When a self becomes lost in possibility in this way, it is not merely because of a lack of energy; at least it is not to be interpreted in the usual way. What is missing is essentially the power to obey, to submit to the necessity in one's life, to what may be called one's limitations. Therefore, the tragedy is not that such a self did not amount to something in the world; no, the tragedy is that he did not become aware of himself, aware that the self he is is a very definite something and thus the necessary. Instead, he lost himself, because this self fantastically reflected itself in possibility. Even in seeing one*self* in a mirror it is necessary to recognize oneself, for if one does not, one does not see one*self* but only a human being. The mirror of possibility is no ordinary mirror; it must be used with extreme caution, for, in the highest sense, this mirror does not tell the truth. That a self appears to be such and such in the possibility of itself is only a half-truth, for in the possibility of itself the self is still far from or is only half of itself. Therefore, the question is how the necessity of this particular self defines it more specifically. Possibility is like a child's invitation to a party; the child is willing at once, but the question now is whether the parents will give permission—and as it is with the parents, so it is with necessity.

XI
150

In possibility everything is possible. For this reason, it is possible to become lost in possibility in all sorts of ways, but primarily in two. The one takes the form of desiring, craving; the other takes the form of the melancholy-imaginary (hope/fear or anxiety). Legends and fairy tales tell of the knight who suddenly sees a rare bird and chases after it, because it seems at first to be very close; but it flies again, and when night comes, he finds himself separated from his companions and lost in the wilderness where he now is. So it is also with desire's possibility. Instead of taking the possibility back into necessity, he chases after possibility—and at last cannot find his way back to himself. —In melancholy the opposite takes place in much the same way. Melancholically enamored, the individual pursues one of anxiety's possibilities, which finally leads him away from himself so that he is a victim of anxiety or a victim of that about which he was anxious lest he be overcome.[36]

β. *Necessity's Despair Is to Lack Possibility*

XI
150

If losing oneself in possibility may be compared with a child's utterance of vowel sounds, then lacking possibility would be the same as being dumb. The necessary is like pure consonants, but to express them there must be possibility. If this is lacking, if a human existence is brought to the point where it lacks possibility, then it is in despair and is in despair every moment it lacks possibility.

Generally it is thought that there is a certain age that is especially rich in hope, or we say that at a certain time, at a particular moment of life, one is or was so rich in hope and possibility. All this, however, is merely a human manner of speaking that does not get at the truth; all this hope and all this despair are as yet neither authentic hope nor authentic despair.

XI
151

What is decisive is that with God everything is possible.[37] This is eternally true and consequently true at every moment. This is indeed a generally recognized truth, which is commonly expressed in this way, but the critical decision does not come until a person is brought to his extremity, when, humanly speaking, there is no possibility. Then the question is whether he will believe that for God everything is possible, that is, whether he will *believe*. But this is the very formula for losing the understanding; to believe is indeed to lose the understanding in order to gain God. Take this analogy. Imagine that someone with a capacity to imagine terrifying nightmares has pictured to himself some horror or other that is absolutely unbearable. Then it happens to him, this very horror happens to him. Humanly speaking, his collapse is altogether certain—and in despair his soul's despair fights to be permitted to despair, to attain, if you please, the composure to despair, to obtain the total personality's consent to despair and be in despair; [38]consequently, there is nothing or no one he would curse more than an attempt or the person making an attempt to hinder him from despairing, as the poet's poet so splendidly and incomparably expresses it (*Richard II*, III, 3):

> *Verwünscht sei Vetter, der mich abgelenkt*
> *Von dem bequemen Wege zur Verzweiflung.*
> [Beshrew thee, cousin, which didst lead me forth
> Of that sweet way I was in to despair!]

At this point, then, salvation is, humanly speaking, utterly impossible; but for God everything is possible! This is the battle of *faith*, battling, madly, if you will, for possibility, because possibility is the only salvation. When someone faints, we call for water, eau de Cologne, smelling salts; but when someone wants to despair, then the word is: Get possibility, get possibility, possibility is the only salvation. A possibility—then the person in despair breathes again, he revives again, for without possibility a person seems unable to breathe. At times the ingeniousness of the human imagination can extend to the point of creating possibility, but at last—that is, when it depends upon *faith*—then only this helps: that for God everything is possible.[39]

And so the struggle goes on. Whether or not the embattled one collapses depends solely upon whether he obtains possibility, that is, whether he will believe. And yet he understands that, humanly speaking, his collapse is altogether certain. This is the dialectic of believing. As a rule, a person knows only that this and that probably, most likely, etc. will not happen to him. If it does happen, it will be his downfall. The foolhardy person rushes headlong into a danger with this or that possibility, and if it happens, he despairs and collapses. The *believer* sees and understands his downfall, humanly speaking (in what has happened to him, or in what he has ventured), but he believes. For this reason he does not collapse. He leaves it entirely to God how he is to be helped, but he believes that for God everything is possible. To *believe* his downfall is impossible. To understand that humanly it is his downfall and nevertheless to believe in possibility is to believe. So God helps him also—perhaps by allowing him to avoid the horror, perhaps through the horror itself—and here, unexpectedly, miraculously, divinely, help does come. Miraculously, for it is a peculiar kind of pedantry to maintain that only 1,800 years ago did it happen that a person was aided miraculously. Whether a person is helped miraculously depends essentially upon the passion of the understanding whereby he has understood that help was impossible and depends next on how honest he was toward the power that nevertheless did help him. As a rule, however, men do neither the one nor the other; they cry out that help is impossible without once straining their understanding to find help, and afterward they ungratefully lie.

The believer has the ever infallible antidote for despair—possibility—because for God everything is possible at every

XI
152

moment. This is the good health of faith that resolves contradictions. The contradiction here is that, humanly speaking, downfall is certain, but that there is possibility nonetheless. Good health generally means the ability to resolve contradictions. For example, in the realm of the bodily or physical, a draft is a contradiction, for a draft is disparately or undialectically cold and warm, but a good healthy body resolves this contradiction and does not notice the draft. So also with faith.

To lack possibility means either that everything has become necessary for a person or that everything has become trivial.

The determinist, the fatalist, is in despair and as one in despair has lost his self, because for him everything has become necessity. He is like that king who starved to death because all his food was changed to gold.[40] Personhood is a synthesis of possibility and necessity. Its continued existence is like breathing (*re*spiration), which is an inhaling and exhaling. The self of the determinist cannot breathe, for it is impossible to breathe necessity exclusively, because that would utterly suffocate a person's self. The fatalist is in despair, has lost God and thus his self, for he who does not have a God does not have a self, either. But the fatalist has no God, or, what amounts to the same thing, his God is necessity; since everything is possible for God, then God is this—that everything is possible. Therefore the fatalist's worship of God is at most an interjection, and essentially it is a muteness, a mute capitulation: he is unable to pray. To pray is also to breathe, and possibility is for the self what oxygen is for breathing. Nevertheless, possibility alone or necessity alone can no more be the condition for the breathing of prayer than oxygen alone or nitrogen[41] alone can be that for breathing. For prayer there must be a God, a self—and possibility—or a self and possibility in a pregnant sense, because the being of God means that everything is possible, or that everything is possible means the being of God; only he whose being has been so shaken that he has become spirit by understanding that everything is possible, only he has anything to do with God. That God's will is the possible makes me able to pray; if there is nothing but necessity, man is essentially as inarticulate as the animals.

It is quite different with the philistine-bourgeois mentality, that is, triviality, which also essentially lacks possibility. The philistine-bourgeois mentality is spiritlessness; determinism and fatalism are despair of spirit, but spiritlessness is also despair. The philistine-bourgeois mentality lacks every qualification of spirit and is completely wrapped up in probability, within which possibility finds its small corner; therefore it lacks the possibility of becoming aware of God. Bereft of imagination, as the philistine-bourgeois always is, whether alehouse keeper or prime minister, he lives within a certain trivial compendium of experiences as to how things go, what is possible, what usually happens. In this way, the philistine-bourgeois has lost his self and God. In order for a person to become aware of his self and of God, imagination must raise him higher than the miasma of probability, it must tear him out of this and teach him to hope and to fear—or to fear and to hope—by rendering possible that which surpasses the *quantum satis* [sufficient amount] of any experience. But the philistine-bourgeois mentality does not have imagination, does not want to have it, abhors it. So there is no help to be had here. And if at times existence provides frightful experiences that go beyond the parrot-wisdom of routine experience, then the philistine-bourgeois mentality despairs, then it becomes apparent that it was despair; it lacks faith's possibility of being able under God to save a self from certain downfall.

Fatalism and determinism, however, do have sufficient imagination to despair of possibility, sufficient possibility to discover impossibility; the philistine-bourgeois mentality reassures itself with the trite and obvious and is just as much in despair whether things go well or badly. Fatalism and determinism lack possibility for the relaxing and mitigating, for the tempering of necessity, and thus lack possibility as mitigation. The philistine-bourgeois mentality thinks that it controls possibility, that it has tricked this prodigious elasticity into the trap or madhouse of probability, thinks that it holds it

XI
154

prisoner; it leads possibility around imprisoned in the cage of probability, exhibits it, imagines itself to be the master, does not perceive that precisely thereby it has imprisoned itself in the thralldom of spiritlessness and is the most wretched of all. The person who gets lost in possibility soars high with the boldness of despair; he for whom everything became necessity overstrains himself in life and is crushed in despair; but the philistine-bourgeois mentality spiritlessly triumphs.

B.
DESPAIR[42] AS DEFINED BY CONSCIOUSNESS

The ever increasing intensity of despair depends upon the degree of consciousness or is proportionate to its increase: the greater the degree of consciousness, the more intensive the despair. This is everywhere apparent, most clearly in despair at its maximum and minimum. The devil's despair is the most intensive despair, for the devil is sheer spirit and hence unqualified consciousness and transparency; there is no obscurity in the devil that could serve as a mitigating excuse. Therefore, his despair is the most absolute defiance. This is despair at its maximum. Despair at its minimum is a state that—yes,
one could humanly be tempted almost to say that in a kind of innocence it does not even know that it is despair. There is the least despair when this kind of unconsciousness is greatest; it is almost a dialectical issue whether it is justifiable to call such a state despair.[43]

a. *The Despair That Is Ignorant of Being Despair, or the Despairing Ignorance of Having a Self and an Eternal Self*

That this condition is nevertheless despair and is properly designated as such manifests what in the best sense of the word may be called the obstinacy of truth. *Veritas est index sui et falsi* [Truth is the criterion of itself and of the false].[44] But this obstinacy of truth certainly is not respected; likewise, it is far from being the case that men regard the relationship to truth, relating themselves to the truth, as the highest good, and it is very far from being the case that they Socratically regard being in error in this manner as the worst misfortune[45]—the sensate in them usually far outweighs their intellectuality. For example, if a man is presumably happy, imagines himself to be happy, although considered in the light of truth he is unhappy, he is usually far from wanting to be wrenched out of his error. On the contrary, he becomes indignant, he regards anyone who does so as his worst enemy, he regards it as an assault bordering on murder in the sense that, as is said, it murders his happiness. Why? Because he is completely dominated by the sensate and the sensate-psychical, because he lives in sensate categories, the pleasant and the unpleasant, waves goodbye to spirit, truth, etc., because he is too sensate to have the courage to venture out and to endure being spirit. However vain and conceited men may be, they usually have a very meager conception of themselves nevertheless, that is, they have no conception of being spirit, the absolute that a human being can be; but vain and conceited they are—on the basis of comparison. Imagine a house with a basement, first floor, and second floor planned so that there is or is supposed to be a social distinction between the occupants according to floor. Now, if what it means to be a human being is compared with such a house, then all too regrettably the sad and ludicrous truth about the majority of people is that in their own house they prefer to live in the basement. Every human being is a psychical-physical synthesis intended to be spirit; this is the building, but he prefers to live in the basement, that is, in sensate categories. Moreover, he not only prefers to live in the basement—no, he loves it so much that he is indignant if anyone suggests that he move to the superb upper floor that stands vacant and at his disposal, for he is, after all, living in his own house.

    No, to be in error is, quite un-Socratically, what men fear least of all.[46] There are amazing examples that amply illustrate this. A thinker erects a huge building, a system, a system embracing the whole of existence, world history, etc., and if his personal life is considered, to our amazement the appalling and ludicrous discovery is made that he himself does not personally live in this huge, domed palace but in a shed alongside

XI
156

it, or in a doghouse, or at best in the janitor's quarters. Were he to be reminded of this contradiction by a single word, he would be insulted. For he does not fear to be in error if he can only complete the system—with the help of being in error.

Therefore, it makes no difference whether the person in despair is ignorant that his condition is despair—he is in despair just the same. If the despair is perplexity [*Forvildelse*], then the ignorance of despair simply adds error [*Vildfarelse*] to it. The relation between ignorance and despair is similar to that between ignorance and anxiety (see *The Concept of Anxiety*[47] by Vigilius Haufniensis); the anxiety that characterizes spiritlessness is recognized precisely by its spiritless sense of security. Nevertheless, anxiety lies underneath; likewise, despair also lies underneath, and when the enchantment of illusion is over, when existence begins to totter, then despair, too, immediately appears as that which lay underneath.

Compared with the person who is conscious of his despair, the despairing individual who is ignorant of his despair is simply a negativity further away from the truth and deliverance. Despair itself is a negativity; ignorance of it, a new negativity. However, to reach the truth, one must go through every negativity, for the old legend about breaking a certain magic spell is true: the piece has to be played through backwards or the spell is not broken.[48] However, it is in only one sense, in a purely dialectic sense, that the individual who is ignorant of his despair is further from the truth and deliverance than one who knows it and yet remains in despair, for in another sense, an ethical-dialectical sense, the person who is conscious of his despair and remains in it is further from deliverance, because his despair is more intensive. Yet ignorance is so far from breaking the despair or changing despair to nondespair that it can in fact be the most dangerous form of despair. To his own demoralization, the individual who in ignorance is in despair is in a way secured against becoming aware—that is, he is altogether secure in the power of despair.

An individual is furthest from being conscious of himself as spirit when he is ignorant of being in despair. But precisely this—not to be conscious of oneself as spirit—is despair, which is spiritlessness, whether the state is a thoroughgoing moribundity, a merely vegetative life, or an intense, energetic life, the secret of which is still despair. In the latter case, the individual in despair is like the consumptive: when the illness is most critical, he feels well, considers himself to be in excellent health, and perhaps seems to others to radiate health.

This form of despair (ignorance of it) is the most common in the world; indeed, what we call the world, or, more exactly, what Christianity calls the world—paganism and the natural man in Christendom, paganism as it was historically and is (and paganism in Christendom is precisely this kind of despair) is despair but is ignorant of the fact. To be sure, paganism and likewise the natural man make the distinction between being in despair and not being in despair—that is, they talk about despair as if only some individuals despaired. Nevertheless, this distinction is just as misleading as the distinction that paganism and the natural man make between love and self-love, as if all this love were not essentially self-love. Beyond this misleading distinction, however, paganism and also the natural man cannot possibly go, because to be ignorant of being in despair is the specific feature of despair.

It is easy to see from all this that the esthetic conception of spiritlessness by no means provides the criterion for judging what is despair and what is not, which, incidentally, is quite in order, for if what is spirit cannot be defined esthetically, how can the esthetic answer a question that simply does not exist for it! It would also be very stupid to deny that individual pagans as well as pagan nations *en masse* have accomplished amazing feats that have inspired and also will inspire poets, to deny that paganism boasts examples of what esthetically cannot be admired enough. It would also be foolish to deny that in paganism the natural man can and does lead a life very rich in esthetic enjoyment, using in the most tasteful manner every favor granted him, and even letting art and science serve to heighten, enhance, and refine his pleasure. No, the esthetic category of spiritlessness does not provide the criterion for what is and what is not despair; what must be applied is the ethical-religious category: spirit or, negatively, the lack of

XI
158

spirit, spiritlessness. Every human existence that is not conscious of itself as spirit or conscious of itself before God as spirit, every human existence that does not rest transparently in God but vaguely rests in and merges in some abstract universality (state, nation, etc.) or, in the dark about his self, regards his capacities merely as powers to produce without becoming deeply aware of their source, regards his self, if it is to have intrinsic meaning, as an indefinable something—every such existence, whatever it achieves, be it most amazing, whatever it explains, be it the whole of existence, however intensively it enjoys life esthetically—every such existence is nevertheless despair. That is what the ancient Church Fathers[49] meant when they said that the virtues of the pagans were glittering vices: they meant that the heart of paganism was despair, that paganism was not conscious before God as spirit. That is why the pagan (to cite this as an example, although it touches this whole investigation in a much more profound way) judged suicide with such singular irresponsibility, yes, praised suicide, which for spirit is the most crucial sin, escaping from existence in this way, mutinying against God. The pagan lacked the spirit's definition of a self, and therefore it judged *suicide* [*S e l v mord*: *self*-murder] in that way; and the same pagan who judged suicide in that way passed severe moral judgment on stealing, unchastity, etc. He lacked the point of view for suicide, he lacked the God-relationship and the self; in purely pagan thinking, suicide is neutral, something entirely up to the pleasure of each individual, since it is no one else's business. If an admonition against suicide were to be given from the viewpoint of paganism, it would have to be in the long, roundabout way of showing that suicide violates the relation of obligation to others. The point that suicide is basically a crime against God completely escapes the pagan.[50] Therefore, it cannot be said that the suicide is despair, for such a remark would be a thoughtless hysteron-proteron;[51] but it may be said that such a judging of suicide by the pagan was despair.

Yet there is and remains a difference, and it is a qualitative difference, between paganism in the stricter sense and

XI
159

paganism in Christendom, the distinction that Vigilius Haufniensis[52] pointed out with respect to anxiety, namely, that
paganism does indeed lack spirit but that it still is qualified in
the direction of spirit, whereas paganism in Christendom
lacks spirit in a departure from spirit or in a falling away and
therefore is spiritlessness in the strictest sense.

b. *The Despair That Is Conscious of Being Despair and Therefore*
Is Conscious of Having a Self in Which There Is Something
Eternal and Then either in Despair Does Not Will to Be Itself or in
Despair Wills to Be Itself

XI
159

Here, of course, the distinction must be made as to whether or
not the person who is conscious of his despair has the true
conception of what despair is. Admittedly, he can be quite
correct, according to his own idea of despair, to say that he is
in despair; he may be correct about being in despair, but that
does not mean that he has the true conception of despair. If his
life is considered according to the true conception of despair,
it is possible that one must say: You are basically deeper in
despair than you know, your despair is on an even profounder
level. So it is also with the pagan (to recall the previous reference). When he regarded himself as being in despair by com-
paring himself with others, he was probably correct about his
being in despair but wrong in regarding the others as not
being in despair—that is, he did not have the true conception
of despair.

On the one hand, then, the true conception of despair is in-
dispensable for conscious despair. On the other hand, it is imperative to have clarity about oneself—that is, insofar as
simultaneous clarity and despair are conceivable. To what
extent perfect clarity about oneself as being in despair can be
combined with being in despair, that is, whether this clarity of
knowledge and of self-knowledge might not simply wrench a
person out of despair, make him so afraid of himself that he
would stop being in despair, we will not determine here; we
will not even make an attempt in that direction, since this
whole investigation will be taken up later.[53] Without pursu-
ing the idea to this dialectical extreme, we merely point out

XI
160

here that just as the level of consciousness of what despair is can vary exceedingly, so also can the level of consciousness of one's own state that it is despair. Actual life is too complex merely to point out abstract contrasts such as that between a despair that is completely unaware of being so and a despair that is completely aware of being so. Very often the person in despair probably has a dim idea of his own state, although here again the nuances are myriad. To some degree, he is aware of being in despair, feels it the way a person does who walks around with a physical malady but does not want to acknowledge forthrightly the real nature of the illness. At one moment, he is almost sure that he is in despair; the next moment, his indisposition seems to have some other cause, something outside of himself, and if this were altered, he would not be in despair. Or he may try to keep himself in the dark about his state through diversions and in other ways, for example, through work and busyness as diversionary means, yet in such a way that he does not entirely realize why he is doing it, that it is to keep himself in the dark. Or he may even realize that he is working this way in order to sink his soul in darkness and does it with a certain keen discernment and shrewd calculation, with psychological insight; but he is not, in a deeper sense, clearly conscious of what he is doing, how despairingly he is conducting himself, etc. There is indeed in all darkness and ignorance a dialectical interplay between knowing and willing, and in comprehending a person one may err by accentuating knowing exclusively or willing exclusively.

XI
161   As pointed out earlier, the level of consciousness intensifies the despair. To the extent that a person has the truer conception of despair, if he still remains in despair, and to the extent that he is more clearly conscious of being in despair—to that extent the despair is more intensive. The person who, with a realization that suicide is despair and to that extent with a true conception of the nature of despair, commits suicide is more intensively in despair than one who commits suicide without a clear idea that suicide is despair; conversely, the less true his conception of despair, the less intensive his despair. On the

other hand, a person who with a clearer consciousness of himself (self-consciousness) commits suicide is more intensively in despair than one whose soul, by comparison, is in confusion and darkness.

⁵⁴I shall now examine the two forms of conscious despair in such a way as to point out also a rise in the consciousness of the nature of despair and in the consciousness that one's state is despair, or, what amounts to the same thing and is the salient point, a rise in the consciousness of the self. The opposite to being in despair is to have faith. Therefore, the formula set forth above, which describes a state in which there is no despair at all, is entirely correct, and this formula is also the formula for faith: in relating itself to itself and in willing to be itself, the self rests transparently in the power that established it (cf. A, A).

α. *In Despair Not to Will to Be Oneself:*
Despair in Weakness

XI
161

To call this form despair in weakness already casts a reflection on the second form, β, in despair to will to be oneself. Thus the opposites are only relative. No despair is entirely free of defiance; indeed, the very phrase "not to will to be" implies defiance. On the other hand, even despair's most extreme defiance is never really free of some weakness. So the distinction is only relative. The one form is, so to speak, feminine despair, the other, masculine despair.*

* An occasional psychological observation of actual life will confirm that this idea, which is sound in thought and consequently shall and must prove to be correct, does in fact prove to be correct, and it will confirm that this classification embraces the entire actuality of despair; for only bad temper, not despair, is associated with children, because we are entitled only to assume that the eternal is present in the child κατὰ δύναμιν [potentially], not to demand it of him as of the adult, for whom it holds that he is meant to have it. I am far from denying that women may have forms of masculine despair and, conversely, that men may have forms of feminine despair, but these are exceptions. And of course the ideal is also a rarity, and only ideally is this distinction between masculine and feminine despair altogether true. However much more tender and sensitive woman may be than man, she has neither the egotistical concept of the self nor, in a decisive sense, intellectuality. But the

XI
162

XI
162

(1) DESPAIR OVER THE EARTHLY OR OVER SOMETHING EARTHLY

This is pure immediacy or immediacy containing a quantitative reflection. —Here there is no infinite consciousness of
XI
163
the self, of what despair is, or of the condition as one of de-

---

feminine nature is devotedness, givingness, and it is unfeminine if it is not·
that. Strange to say, no one can be as coy (and this word was coined especially
for women), so almost cruelly hard to please as a woman—and yet by nature
she is devotedness, and (this is precisely the wonder of it) all this actually expresses that her nature is devotedness. For precisely because she carries in her
being this total feminine devotedness, nature has affectionately equipped her
with an instinct so sensitive that by comparison the most superior masculine
reflection is as nothing. This devotedness on the part of woman, this, to speak
as a Greek, divine gift and treasure, is too great a good to be tossed away
blindly, and yet no clear-sighted human reflection is capable of seeing sharply
enough to use it properly. That is why nature has looked after her:
blindfolded, she instinctively sees more clearly than the most clear-sighted
reflection; instinctively she sees what she should admire, that to which she
should give herself. Devotedness is the one unique quality that woman has,
and that is also why nature took it upon itself to be her guardian. That is the
reason, too, why womanliness comes into existence only through a
metamorphosis; it comes into existence when woman's illimitable coyness
expresses itself as feminine devotedness. By nature, however, woman's devotedness also enters into despair, is again a mode of despair. In devotion she
loses herself, and only then is she happy, only then is she herself; a woman
XI
163
who is happy without devotion, that is, ⁵⁵without giving her self, no matter
to what she gives it, is altogether unfeminine. A man also gives himself—and
he is a poor kind of man who does not do so—but his self is not devotion (this
is the expression for feminine substantive devotion), nor does he gain his self
by devotion, as woman in another sense does; he has himself. He gives himself, but his self remains behind as a sober awareness of devotion, whereas
woman, with genuine femininity, abandons herself, throws her self into that
to which she devotes herself. Take this devotion away, then her self is also
gone, and her despair is: not to will to be oneself. The man does not give
himself in this way, but the second form of despair also expresses the masculine form: in despair to will to be oneself.

The above pertains to the relation between masculine and feminine despair.
But it is to be borne in mind that this does not refer to devotion to God or to
the God-relationship, which will be considered in Part Two. In the relationship to God, where the distinction of man-woman vanishes, it holds for men
as well as for women that devotion is the self and that in the giving of oneself
the self is gained. This holds equally for man and woman, although it is probably true that in most cases the woman actually relates to God only through
the man.

spair. The despair is only a suffering, a succumbing to the pressure of external factors; in no way does it come from within as an act. The appearance of such words as "the self" and "despair" in the language of immediacy is due, if you will, to an innocent abuse of language, a playing with words, like the children's game of playing soldier.

The *man of immediacy* is only psychically qualified (insofar as there really can be immediacy without any reflection at all); his self, he himself, is an accompanying something within the dimensions of temporality and secularity, in immediate connection with "the other" (το ἕτερον), and has but an illusory appearance of having anything eternal in it. The self is bound up in immediacy with the other in desiring, craving, enjoying, etc., yet passively; in its craving, this self is a dative, like the "me" of a child. Its dialectic is: the pleasant and the unpleasant; its concepts are: good luck, bad luck, fate.

Now something *happens* that impinges (*upon* + *to strike*) upon this immediate self and makes it despair. In another sense, it cannot happen at this point; since the self has no reflection, there must be an external motivation for the despair, and the despair is nothing more than a submitting. By a "stroke of fate" that which to the man of immediacy is his whole life, or, insofar as he has a minuscule of reflection, the portion thereof to which he especially clings, is taken from him; in short, he becomes, as he calls it, unhappy, that is, his immediacy is dealt such a crushing blow that it cannot reproduce itself: he despairs. Or—and although this is rarely seen in actuality, it is dialectically quite in order—this despair on the part of immediacy is occasioned by what the man of immediacy calls extraordinary good luck, for immediacy as such is so extremely fragile that every *quid nimis* [excess] that requires reflection of it brings it to despair.

So he despairs—that is, in a strange reversal and in complete mystification about himself, he calls it despairing. But to despair is to lose the eternal—and of this loss he does not speak at all, he has no inkling of it. In itself, to lose the things of this world is not to despair; yet this is what he talks about, and this is what he calls despairing. In a certain sense, what he

XI
164

says is true, but not in the way he understands it; he is conversely situated, and what he says must be interpreted conversely: he stands and points to what he calls despair but is not
despair, and in the meantime, sure enough, despair is right
there behind him without his realizing it. It is as if someone
facing away from the town hall and courthouse pointed
straight ahead and said: There is the town hall and courthouse. He is correct, it is there—if he turns around.[56] He is
not in despair—this is not true—and yet he is correct in saying
it. He claims he is in despair, he regards himself as dead, as a
shadow of himself. But dead he is not; there is still, one might
say, life in the person. If everything, all the externals, were to
change suddenly, and if his desire were fulfilled, then there
would be life in him again, then spontaneity and immediacy
would escalate again, and he would begin to live all over
again. This is the only way immediacy knows how to strive,
the only thing it knows: to despair and faint—and yet, that
about which he knows the least is despair. He despairs and
faints, and after that lies perfectly still as if he were dead, a
trick like "playing dead"; immediacy resembles certain lower
animals that have no weapon or means of defense other than
to lie perfectly still and pretend that they are dead.

Meanwhile, time passes. If help arrives from the outside,
the person in despair comes alive again, he begins where he
left off; a self he was not, and a self he did not become, but he
goes on living, qualified only by immediacy. If there is no external help, something else frequently happens in actual life.
In spite of everything, there is still life in the person, but he
says that "he will never be himself again." He now acquires a
little understanding of life, he learns to copy others, how they
manage their lives—and he now proceeds to live the same
way. In Christendom he is also a Christian, goes to church
every Sunday, listens to and understands the pastor, indeed,
they have a mutual understanding; he dies, the pastor ushers
him into eternity for ten rix-dollars—but a self he was not,
and a self he did not become.

This form of despair is: in despair not to will to be oneself.
Or even lower: in despair not to will to be a self. Or lowest of

all: in despair to will to be someone else, to wish for a new self. Immediacy actually has no self, it does not know itself; thus it cannot recognize itself and therefore generally ends in fantasy. When immediacy despairs, it does not even have enough self to wish or dream that it had become that which it has not become. The man of immediacy helps himself in another way: he wishes to be someone else. This is easily verified by observing immediate persons; when they are in despair, there is nothing they desire more than to have been someone else or to become someone else. In any case, it is difficult to keep from smiling at one who despairs in this way, who, humanly speaking and despite being in despair, is so very innocent. As a rule, one who despairs in this way is very comical. Imagine a self (and next to God there is nothing as eternal as a self), and then imagine that it suddenly occurs to a self that it might become someone other—than itself. And yet one in despair this way, whose sole desire is this most lunatic of lunatic metamorphoses, is infatuated with the illusion that this change can be accomplished as easily as one changes clothes. The man of immediacy does not know himself, he quite literally identifies himself only by the clothes he wears, he identifies having a self by externalities (here again the infinitely comical). There is hardly a more ludicrous mistake, for a self is indeed infinitely distinct from an externality. So when the externals have completely changed for the person of immediacy and he has despaired, he goes one step further; he thinks something like this, it becomes his wish: What if I became someone else, got myself a new self. Well, what if he did become someone else? I wonder whether he would recognize himself. There is a story about a peasant who went barefooted to town with enough money to buy himself a pair of stockings and shoes and to get drunk, and in trying to find his way home in his drunken state, he fell asleep in the middle of the road. A carriage came along, and the driver shouted to him to move or he would drive over his legs. The drunken peasant woke up, looked at his legs and, not recognizing them because of the shoes and stockings, said: "Go ahead, they are not my legs." When the man of immediacy despairs, it is impos-

XI
166

sible to give a true description of him outside of the comic; if I may put it this way, it is already something of a feat to speak in that jargon about a self and about despair.

When immediacy is assumed to have some reflection, the despair is somewhat modified; a somewhat greater consciousness of the self comes about, and thereby of the nature of despair and of one's condition as despair. It means something for such an individual to talk about being in despair, but the despair is essentially despair in weakness, a suffering, and its form is: in despair not to will to be oneself.

The advance over pure immediacy manifests itself at once in the fact that despair is not always occasioned by a blow, by something happening, but can be brought on by one's capacity for reflection, so that despair, when it is present, is not merely a suffering, a succumbing to the external circumstance, but is to a certain degree self-activity, an act. A certain degree of reflection is indeed present here, consequently a certain degree of pondering over one's self. With this certain degree of reflection begins the act of separation whereby the self becomes aware of itself as essentially different from the environment and external events and from their influence upon it. But this is only to a certain degree. When the self with a certain degree of reflection in itself wills to be responsible for the self, it may come up against some difficulty or other in the structure of the self, in the self's necessity. For just as no human body is perfect, so no self is perfect. This difficulty, whatever it is, makes him recoil. Or something happens to him that breaks with the immediacy in him more profoundly than his reflection had done, or his imagination discovers a possibility that, if it eventuated, would thus become the break with immediacy.

So he despairs. In contrast to the despair of self-assertion, his despair is despair in weakness, a suffering of the self; but with the aid of the relative reflection that he has, he attempts to sustain his self, and this constitutes another difference from the purely immediate man. He perceives that abandoning the self is a transaction, and thus he does not become apoplectic when the blow falls, as the immediate person does; reflection helps him to understand that there is much he can lose without losing the self. He makes concessions; he is able to do so—and why? Because to a certain degree he has separated his self from externalities, because he has a dim idea that there may even be something eternal in the self. Nevertheless, his struggles are in vain; the difficulty he has run up against requires a total break with immediacy, and he does not have the self-reflection or the ethical reflection for that. He has no consciousness of a self that is won by infinite abstraction from every externality, this naked abstract self, which, compared with immediacy's fully dressed self, is the first form of the infinite self and the advancing impetus in the whole process by which a self infinitely becomes responsible for its actual self with all its difficulties and advantages.

So he despairs, and his despair is: not to will to be himself. But he certainly does not entertain the ludicrous notion of wanting to be someone else; he keeps up the relation to his self—reflection has attached him to the self to that extent. His relation to the self is like the relation a person may have to his place of residence (the comic aspect is that the self certainly does not have as contingent a relation to itself as one has to a place of residence), which becomes an abomination because of smoke fumes or something else, whatever it might be. So he leaves it, but he does not move away, he does not set up a new residence; he continues to regard the old one as his address, he assumes that the problem will disappear. So also with the person in despair. As long as the difficulty lasts, he does not dare, as the saying so trenchantly declares, "to come to himself," he does not will to be himself; presumably this will pass, perhaps a change will take place, this gloomy possibility will probably be forgotten. So as long as it lasts, he visits himself, so to speak, only occasionally, to see whether the change has commenced. As soon as it commences, he moves home again, "is himself once again," as he says; but this simply means that he begins where he left off—he was a self up to a point and he went no further than that.

If there is no change, he seeks another remedy. He turns away completely from the inward way along which he should

XI
168

have advanced in order truly to become a self. In a deeper sense, the whole question of the self becomes a kind of false door with nothing behind it in the background of his soul. He appropriates what he in his language calls his self, that is, whatever capacities, talents, etc. he may have; all these he appropriates but in an outward-bound direction, toward life, as they say, toward the real, the active life. He behaves very discreetly with the little bit of reflection he has within himself, fearing that what he has in the background might emerge again. Little by little, he manages to forget it; in the course of time, he finds it almost ludicrous, especially when he is together with other competent and dynamic men who have a sense and aptitude for real life. Charming! He has been happily married now for several years, as it says in novels, is a dynamic and enterprising man, a father and citizen, perhaps even an important man; at home in his own house the servants call him "He Himself"; downtown he is among those addressed with "His Honor"; his conduct is based on respect of persons or on the way others regard one, and others judge according to one's social position. In Christendom he is a Christian[57] (in the very same sense as in paganism he would be a pagan and in Holland a Hollander), one of the cultured Christians. The question of immortality has often occupied him, and more than once he has asked the pastor whether there is such an immortality, whether one would actually recognize himself again—something that certainly must be of very particular interest to him, since he has no self.

It is impossible to depict this kind of despair accurately without a certain touch of satire. It is comical that he wants to talk about having been in despair; it is appalling that after the conquering of despair, according to his view, his condition is in fact despair. Ideally understood, it is extremely comical that underlying the worldly wisdom that is so celebrated in the world, underlying all that diabolical profusion of good advice and clever clichés—"Wait and see," "Don't worry," "Forget it"—there is utter stupidity about where and what the danger actually is. Again, it is this ethical stupidity that is appalling.

Despair over the earthly or over something earthly is the

most common form of despair, and especially in the second form, that is, immediacy with a quantitative reflection. The more despair is thought through, the more rarely it is seen or the more rarely it appears in the world. This by no means proves that the majority have not despaired; it proves only that they have not gone particularly deep in despairing. There are very few persons who live even approximately within the qualification of spirit; indeed, there are not many who even try this life, and most of those who do soon back out of it. They have not learned to fear, have not learned "to have to" without any dependence, none at all, upon whatever else happens. Therefore, they are unable to bear what already appears to them to be a contradiction, what in reflection in the surroundings looks all the more glaring, so that to be concerned about one's soul and to will to be spirit seems to be a waste of time in the world, indeed, an indefensible waste of time that ought to be punished by civil law if possible, one that is punished in any case with scorn and contempt as a kind of treason against the human race, as a defiant madness that insanely fills out time with nothing. Then comes a moment in their lives—alas, this is their best time—when they begin to turn inward. Then, when they encounter their first difficulties, they turn away; it seems to them that this path leads to a dismal desert—*und rings umher liegt schöne grüne Weide* [while all about lie meadows fresh and green].[58] And so they take off and soon forget that time, the best time of their lives—alas, forget it as if it were a piece of childishness. They are also Christians, reassured by the pastors of their salvation. As stated, this despair is the most common, so common that this alone explains the common notion that despair is part of being young, something that appears only in the early years but is not found in the mature person who has reached the age of discretion. This is a desperate error or, more correctly, a desperate mistake that disregards—yes, and what is even worse, disregards the fact that what it disregards is almost the best that can be said about people, because very often something far worse happens—disregards the fact that, fundamentally, most people virtually never advance beyond what they were in their childhood and youth: immediacy with the admixture of a little dash of reflection. No, despair certainly is not something that appears only in the young, something one outgrows as a matter of course—"just as one outgrows illusion." This is not the case, even though one may be foolish enough to believe it. On the contrary, we can often enough meet men and women and older people who have illusions just as childish as any young person's. We disregard the fact that illusion essentially has two forms: the illusion of hope and the illusion of recollection. Youth has the illusion of hope; the adult has the illusion of recollection, but precisely because he has this illusion, he also has the utterly biased idea of illusion that there is only the illusion of hope. The adult, of course, is not troubled by the illusion of hope but instead by the quaint illusion, among others, of looking down on the illusions of youth, presumably from a higher point free of illusion. The youth has illusions, hopes for something extraordinary from life and from himself; the adult, in recompense, is often found to have illusions about his memories of his youth. An older woman who presumably has left all illusions behind her is often found to be just as fantastically deluded as any young girl when it comes to her recollection of herself as a young girl, how happy she was then, how beautiful, etc. This *fuimus* [we have been],[59] which is common to older people, is just as great an illusion as the illusions of young people about the future: they both lie or fictionalize.

The mistaken notion that despair belongs only to youth is also desperate and despairing in quite another way. Moreover, it is very foolish and simply shows a lack of judgment as to what spirit is—along with a failure to appreciate that man is spirit and not merely animal—to think that faith and wisdom come that easily, that they come as a matter of course over the years like teeth, a beard, etc. No, whatever a man may arrive at as a matter of course, whatever things may come as a matter of course—faith and wisdom are definitely not among them. As a matter of fact, from a spiritual point of view, a man does not arrive at anything as a matter of course over the years; this concept is precisely the uttermost opposite of spirit. On the contrary, it is very easy to leave something be- _{XI} ₁₇₁ hind as a matter of course over the years. And over the years, an individual may abandon the little bit of passion, feeling, imagination, the little bit of inwardness he had and embrace as a matter of course an understanding of life in terms of triv- ialities (for such things come as a matter of course). This— improved—condition, which, to be sure, has come with the years, he now in despair considers a good thing; he easily reassures himself (and in a certain satirical sense nothing is more sure) that now it could never occur to him to despair— no, he has secured himself. But he is in despair, devoid of spirit and in despair. Why, I wonder, did Socrates love youth if it was not because he knew man!

If over the years an individual does not happen to sink into this most trivial kind of despair, it still by no means follows that despair belongs merely to youth. If a person really does develop over the years, if he becomes mature in an essential consciousness of the self, then he may despair in a higher form. And if he does not develop essentially over the years, although he still does not sink completely into triviality—that is, if he never advances any further than being a young man, a youth, even though he is an adult, a father, and a gray-head, consequently retaining some of the good in youth—he will be just as liable as a youth to despair over the earthly or over something earthly.

There may well be a difference between the despair of an adult like that and a youth's despair, but it is purely incidental, nothing essential. The youth despairs over the future as the present *in futuro* [in the future]; there is something in the fu- ture that he is not willing to take upon himself, and therefore he does not will to be himself. The adult despairs over the past as a present *in præterito* [in the past] that refuses to recede fur- ther into the past, for his despair is not such that he has suc- ceeded in forgetting it completely. This past may even be something that repentance really should have in custody. But if repentance is to arise, there must first be effective despair, radical despair, so that the life of the spirit can break through from the ground upward. But in despair as he is, he does not dare to let it come to such a decision. There he stands still, time passes—unless, even more in despair, he succeeds in healing it by forgetting it, and thus instead of becoming a penitent, he becomes his own receiver of stolen goods [*Hæler*].[60] But essentially the despair of a youth and of an adult remains the same; there is never a metamorphosis in which consciousness of the eternal in the self breaks through so that the battle can begin that either intensifies the despair in a still higher form or leads to faith.

Is there, then, no essential difference between the two expressions used identically up to now: to despair over the earthly (the category of totality) and to despair over something earthly (the particular)? Indeed there is. When the self in imagination despairs with infinite passion over something of this world, its infinite passion changes this particular thing, this something, into the world *in toto*; that is, the category of totality inheres in and belongs to the despairing person. The earthly and the temporal as such are precisely that which falls apart or disintegrates into particulars, into some particular thing. The loss or deprivation of every earthly thing is actually impossible, for the category of totality is a thought category. Consequently, the self infinitely magnifies the actual loss and then despairs over the earthly *in toto*. However, as soon as this distinction (between despairing over the earthly and over something earthly) must be maintained essentially, there is also an essential advance in consciousness of the self. This formula, to despair over the earthly, is then a dialectical initial expression for the next form of despair.

(2) DESPAIR OF THE ETERNAL OR OVER ONESELF[61]

Despair over the earthly or over something earthly is in reality also despair of the eternal and over oneself, insofar as it is despair, for this is indeed the formula for all despair.*

* And therefore it is linguistically correct to say: to despair *over* the earthly (the occasion), *of* the eternal, but *over* oneself. For this again is another expression for the occasion of despair, which, according to the concept, is always *of* the eternal, whereas *that which* is despaired *over* can be very diverse.[62] We de-

spair *over* that which binds us in despair—over a misfortune, over the earthly,

But the individual in despair depicted above is not aware, XI 173 so to speak, of what is going on behind him. He thinks he is despairing over something earthly and talks constantly of that over which he despairs, and yet he is despairing of the eternal, for the fact that he attributes such great worth to something earthly—or, to carry this further, that he attributes to something earthly such great worth, or that he first makes something earthly into the whole world and then attributes such great worth to the earthly—this is in fact to despair of the eternal.

This despair is a significant step forward. If the preceding despair was *despair in weakness*, then this is *despair over his weakness*, while still remaining within the category: despair in weakness as distinct from despair in defiance (β). Consequently, there is only a relative difference, namely, that the previous form has weakness's consciousness as its final consciousness, whereas here the consciousness does not stop with that but rises to a new consciousness—that of his weakness. The person in despair himself understands that it is weakness to make the earthly so important, that it is weakness to despair. But now, instead of definitely turning away from despair to faith and humbling himself under his weakness, he entrenches himself in despair and despairs over his weakness. In so doing, his whole point of view is turned around: he now becomes more clearly conscious of his despair, that he despairs of the eternal, that he despairs over himself, over being so weak that he attributes such great significance to the earthly, which now becomes for him the despairing sign that he has lost the eternal and himself.

---

over a capital loss, etc.—but we despair *of* that which, rightly understood, releases us from despair: of the eternal, of salvation, of our own strength, etc. With respect to the self, we say both: to despair *over* and *of* oneself, because the self is doubly dialectical. And the haziness, particularly in all the lower forms of despair and in almost every person in despair, is that he so passionately and clearly sees and knows *over* what he despairs, but *of* what he despairs evades him. The condition for healing is always this repenting *of*, and, purely philosophically, it could be a subtle question whether it is possible for one to be in despair and be fully aware of that *of* which one despairs.

The progression is as follows. First comes the consciousness of the self, for to despair of the eternal is impossible without having a conception of the self, that there is something eternal in it, or that it has had something eternal in it.

If a person is to despair over himself, he must be aware of having a self; and yet it is over this that he despairs, not over the earthly or something earthly, but over himself. Furthermore, there is a greater consciousness here of what despair is, because despair is indeed the loss of the eternal and of oneself. Of course, there is also a greater consciousness that one's state is despair. Then, too, despair here is not merely a suffering but an act. When the world is taken away from the self and one despairs, the despair seems to come from the outside, even though it always comes from the self; but when the self despairs over its despair, this new despair comes from the self, indirectly-directly from the self, as the counter-pressure (reaction), and it thereby differs from defiance, which comes directly from the self. Ultimately, this is still a step forward, although in another sense; simply because this despair is more intensive, it is in a certain sense closer to salvation. It is difficult to forget such despair—it is too deep; but every minute that despair is kept open, there is the possibility of salvation as well.

Nevertheless, this despair is classified under the form: in despair not to will to be oneself. Like a father who disinherits a son, the self does not want to acknowledge itself after having been so weak. In despair it cannot forget this weakness; it hates itself in a way, will not in faith humble itself under its weakness in order thereby to recover itself—no, in despair it does not wish, so to speak, to hear anything about itself, does not itself know anything to say. Nor is there any question of being helped by forgetting or of slipping, by means of forgetting, into the category of the spiritless and then to be a man and a Christian like other men and Christians—no, for that the self is too much self. As is often the case with the father who disinherits his son, the external circumstance is of little help; he does not thereby rid himself of his son, at least not in his thought. It is often the case when a lover curses the one he detests (his beloved) that it does not help very much; it captivates him almost more—and so it goes with the despairing self in regard to itself.

This despair is qualitatively a full level deeper than the one described earlier and belongs to the despair that less frequently appears in the world. That false door mentioned previously, behind which there is nothing, is here a real door, but a carefully closed door, and behind it sits the self, so to speak, watching itself, preoccupied with or filling up time with not willing to be itself and yet being self enough to love itself. This is called inclosing reserve [*Indesluttethed*]. And from now on we shall discuss inclosing reserve, which is the very opposite of immediacy and in terms of thought, among other things, has a great contempt for it.

XI
175

Is there no one with such a self in the world of actuality, has he taken flight from actuality into the desert, the monastery, the madhouse; is he not an actual human being, dressed like others, wearing ordinary outer garments? Of course, why not! But this matter of the self he shares with no one, not a soul; he feels no urge to do so, or he has learned to subdue it. Just listen to what he himself says of it: "In fact, it is only purely immediate man—who in the category of spirit is just about on the same level as the young child, who, with utterly lovable unconstraint, tells all—it is only purely immediate people who are unable to hold anything back. It is this kind of immediacy that often with great pretension calls itself 'truth, being honest, an honest man telling it exactly as it is,' and this is just as much a truth as it is an untruth when an adult does not immediately yield to a physical urge. Every self with just a minuscule of reflection still knows how to constrain the self." And our man in despair is sufficiently self-inclosed to keep this matter of the self away from anyone who has no business knowing about it—in other words, everyone—while outwardly he looks every bit "a real man." He is a university graduate, husband, father, even an exceptionally

competent public officeholder, a respectable father, pleasant company, very gentle to his wife, solicitude personified
to his children. And Christian? —Well, yes, he is that, too,
but prefers not to talk about it, although with a certain
wistful joy he likes to see that his wife is occupied with
religion to her upbuilding. He rarely attends church, because he feels that most pastors really do not know what
they are talking about. He makes an exception of one particular pastor and admits that he knows what he is talking
about, but he has another reason for not wanting to listen
to him, since he fears being led too far out. On the other
hand, he not infrequently longs for solitude, which for him
is a necessity of life, at times like the necessity to breathe, at
other times like the necessity to sleep. That this is a life-
necessity for him more than for most people also manifests
his deeper nature. On the whole, the longing for solitude is

a sign that there still is spirit in a person and is the measure
of what spirit there is. "Utterly superficial nonpersons and
group-people" feel such a meager need for solitude that, like
lovebirds, they promptly die the moment they have to be
alone. Just as a little child has to be lulled to sleep, so these
people need the soothing lullaby of social life in order to be
able to eat, drink, sleep, fall in love, etc. In antiquity as well
as in the Middle Ages there was an awareness of this longing
for solitude and a respect for what it means; whereas in the
constant sociality of our day we shrink from solitude to the
point (what a capital epigram!) that no use for it is known
other than as a punishment for criminals. But since it is a
crime in our day to have spirit, it is indeed quite in order to
classify such people, lovers of solitude, with criminals.

The self-inclosing despairing person goes on living *horis
succesivis* [hour after hour]; even if not lived for eternity,[63] his
hours have something to do with the eternal and are concerned with the relation of his self to itself—but he never really gets beyond that. When it is done, when his longing for
solitude is satisfied, he goes out, as it were—even when he
goes in to or is involved with his wife and children. Aside

from his natural good nature and sense of duty, what makes him such a kind husband and solicitous father is the confession about his weakness that he has made to himself in his inclosed innermost being.

If it were possible for anyone to share the secret of his inclosing reserve and if one were then to say to him, "It is pride, you are really proud of yourself," he probably would never make the confession to anyone else. Alone with himself, he no doubt would confess that there is something to it, but the passionateness with which his self has interpreted his weakness would soon lead him into believing that it cannot possibly be pride, because it is indeed his very weakness that he despairs over—just as if it were not pride that places such tremendous emphasis on the weakness, just as if it were not because he wants to be proud of his self that he cannot bear this consciousness of weakness. —If someone were to say to him, "This is a curious entanglement, a curious kind of knot, for the whole trouble is really the way your thinking twists around; otherwise it is even normal, in fact, this is precisely the course you have to take: you must go through the despair of the self to the self.[64] You are quite right about the weakness, but that is not what you are to despair over; the self must be broken in order to become itself, but quit despairing over that"—if someone were to speak that way to him, he would understand it in a dispassionate moment, but his passion would soon see mistakenly again, and then once more he would make a wrong turn—into despair.

XI
177

As stated, this kind of despair is quite rare in the world. If it does not stop there and just mark time on the spot, and if on the other hand the person in despair does not experience an upheaval that puts him on the right road to faith, despair of this kind will either become intensified in a higher form of despair and continue to be inclosing reserve, or it will break through and destroy the outward trappings in which such a despairing person has been living out his life as if in an incognito. In the latter case, a person in this kind of despair will hurl himself into life, perhaps into the diversion of great enterprises; he will become a restless spirit whose life certainly leaves its mark, a restless spirit who wants to forget, and when the internal tumult is too much for him, he has to take strong measures, although of another kind than Richard III used in order not to hear his mother's curses.[65] Or he will seek oblivion in sensuality, perhaps in dissolute living; in despair he wants to go back to immediacy, but always with the consciousness of the self he does not want to be. In the first case, if the despair is intensified, it becomes defiance, and it now becomes clear how much untruth there was in this whole matter of weakness—it becomes clear how dialectically correct it is that the first expression for defiance is this very despair over his weakness.

In conclusion, let us take still another little look at the person of inclosing reserve who in his inclosing reserve marks time on the spot. If this inclosing reserve is maintained completely, *omnibus numeris absoluta* [completely in every respect], then his greatest danger is suicide. Most men, of course, have no intimation of what such a person of inclosing reserve can endure; if they knew, they would be amazed. The danger, then, for the completely inclosed person is suicide. But if he opens up to one single person, he probably will become so relaxed, or so let down, that suicide will not result from inclosing reserve. Such a person of inclosing reserve with one confidant is moderated by one whole tone in comparison with one who is fully inclosed. Presumably he will avoid suicide. However, it may happen that just because he has opened himself to another person he will despair over having done so; it may seem to him that he might have held out far, far longer in silence rather than to have a confidant. There are examples of persons of inclosing reserve who were thrown into despair by having found a confidant. In this way, suicide may still result. In a poetic treatment, the denouement (assuming *poetice* [poetically] that the person was, for example, a king or an emperor) could be designed so that the confidant is killed. It is possible to imagine a demonic tyrant like that, one who craves to speak with someone about his torment and then successively consumes a considerable number of people, for to become his confidant means certain death: as soon as the tyrant has spoken in his presence, he is put to death. —It would be a task for a poet to depict this solution to a demoniac's tormenting self-contradiction: not to be able to do without a confidant and not to be able to have a confidant.[66]

β. *In Despair to Will to Be Oneself: Defiance*

As pointed out, the despair in α could be called feminine; similarly, this despair may be called masculine. It is, therefore, in relation to the foregoing, despair considered within the qualification of spirit. So perceived, however, masculinity essentially belongs within the qualification of spirit, while femininity is a lower synthesis.

The kind of despair described in α(2) was over one's weakness; the despairing individual does not will to be himself. But if the person in despair goes one single dialectical step further, if he realizes why he does not will to be himself, then there is a shift, then there is defiance, and this is the case precisely because in despair he wills to be himself.

First comes despair over the earthly or over something earthly, then despair of the eternal, over oneself. Then comes defiance, which is really despair through the aid of the eternal, the despairing misuse of the eternal within the self to will in despair to be oneself. But just because it is despair through the aid of the eternal, in a certain sense it is very close to the truth; and just because it lies very close to the truth, it is infinitely far away. The despair that is the thoroughfare to faith comes also through the aid of the eternal; through the aid of the eternal the self has the courage to lose itself in order to win itself. Here, however, it is unwilling to begin with losing itself but wills to be itself.

In this form of despair, there is a rise in the consciousness of the self, and therefore a greater consciousness of what despair is and that one's state is despair. Here the despair is conscious of itself as an act; it does not come from the outside as a suffering under the pressure of externalities but comes directly from the self. Therefore defiance, compared with despair over one's weakness, is indeed a new qualification.

In order in despair to will to be oneself, there must be con-

XI
178

XI
179

sciousness of an infinite self. This infinite self, however, is really only the most abstract form, the most abstract possibility of the self. And this is the self that a person in despair wills to be, severing the self from any relation to a power that has established it, or severing it from the idea that there is such a power. With the help of this infinite form, the self in despair wants to be master of itself or to create itself, to make his self into the self he wants to be, to determine what he will have or not have in his concrete self. His concrete self or his concretion certainly has necessity and limitations, is this very specific being with these natural capacities, predispositions, etc. in this specific concretion of relations etc. But with the help of the infinite form, the negative self, he wants first of all to take upon himself the transformation of all this in order to fashion out of it a self such as he wants, produced with the help of the infinite form of the negative self—and in this way he wills to be himself. In other words, he wants to begin a little earlier than do other men, not at and with the beginning, but "in the beginning";[67] he does not want to put on his own self, does not want to see his given self as his task—he himself wants to compose his self by means of being the infinite form.

If a generic name for this despair is wanted, it could be called stoicism, but understood as not referring only to that sect. To elucidate this kind of despair more precisely, it is best to distinguish between an acting self and a self acted upon and to show how the self, when it is acting, relates itself to itself, and how the self, when it is acted upon, in being affected, relates itself to itself—and thus to show that the formula always is: in despair to will to be oneself.

XI
180 If the self in despair is an *acting self*, it constantly relates itself to itself only by way of imaginary constructions, no matter what it undertakes, however vast, however amazing, however perseveringly pursued. It recognizes no power over itself; therefore it basically lacks earnestness and can conjure forth only an appearance of earnestness, even when it gives its utmost attention to its imaginary constructions. This is a simulated earnestness. Like Prometheus stealing fire from the gods, this is stealing from God the thought—which is ear-

nestness—that God pays attention to one; instead, the self in despair is satisfied with paying attention to itself, which is supposed to bestow infinite interest and significance upon his enterprises, but it is precisely this that makes them imaginary constructions. For even if this self does not go so far into despair that it becomes an imaginatively constructed god—no derived self can give itself more than it is in itself by paying attention to itself—it remains itself from first to last; in its self-redoubling it becomes neither more nor less than itself. In so far as the self in its despairing striving to be itself works itself into the very opposite, it really becomes no self. In the whole dialectic within which it acts there is nothing steadfast; at no moment is the self steadfast, that is, eternally steadfast. The negative form of the self exercises a loosening power as well as a binding power;[68] at any time it can quite arbitrarily start all over again, and no matter how long one idea is pursued, the entire action is within a hypothesis. The self is so far from successfully becoming more and more itself that the fact merely becomes increasingly obvious that it is a hypothetical self. The self is its own master, absolutely its own master, so-called; and precisely this is the despair, but also what it regards as its pleasure and delight. On closer examination, however, it is easy to see that this absolute ruler is a king without a country, actually ruling over nothing; his position, his sovereignty, is subordinate to the dialectic that rebellion is legitimate at any moment. Ultimately, this is arbitrarily based upon the self itself.

Consequently, the self in despair is always building only castles in the air, is only shadowboxing. All these imaginatively constructed virtues make it look splendid; like oriental poetry, they fascinate for a moment; such self-command, such imperturbability, such ataraxia, etc. practically border on the fabulous. Yes, they really do, and the basis of the whole thing is nothing. In despair the self wants to enjoy the total satisfaction of making itself into itself, of developing itself, of being itself; it wants to have the honor of this poetic, masterly construction, the way it has understood itself. And yet, in the final analysis, what it understands by itself is a riddle; in the

XI
181

very moment when it seems that the self is closest to having the building completed, it can arbitrarily dissolve the whole thing into nothing.[69]

If the self in despair is *acted upon*, the despair is nevertheless: in despair to will to be oneself. Perhaps such an imaginatively constructing self, which in despair wills to be itself, encounters some difficulty or other while provisionally orienting itself to its concrete self, something the Christian would call a cross, a basic defect, whatever it may be. The negative self, the infinite form of the self, will perhaps reject this completely, pretend that it does not exist, will having nothing to do with it. But it does not succeed; its proficiency in imaginary constructing does not stretch that far, and not even its proficiency in abstracting does. In a Promethean way, the infinite, negative self feels itself nailed to this servitude. Consequently, it is a self acted upon. What, then, are the manifestations of this despair that is: in despair to will to be oneself?

In the preceding pages, the form of despair that despairs over the earthly or something earthly was understood basically to be—and it also manifests itself as being—despair of the eternal, that is, an unwillingness to be comforted by and healed by the eternal, an overestimation of the things of this world to the extent that the eternal can be no consolation. But this is also a form of the despair, to be unwilling to hope in the possibility that an earthly need, a temporal cross, can come to an end. The despairing person who in despair wills to be himself is unwilling to do that. He has convinced himself that this thorn in the flesh[70] gnaws so deeply that he cannot abstract himself from it (whether this is actually the case or his passion makes it so to him*), and therefore he might as well accept it

---

* Moreover, lest it be overlooked, from this point of view one will see that much of what in the world is dressed up under the name of resignation is a kind of despair: in despair to will to be one's abstract self, in despair to will to make the eternal suffice, and thereby to be able to defy or ignore suffering in the earthly and the temporal. The dialectic of resignation is essentially this: to will to be one's eternal self and then, when it comes to something specific in which the self suffers, not to will to be oneself, taking consolation in the thought that it may disappear in eternity and therefore feeling justified in not accepting it in time. Although suffering under it, the self will still not make

forever, so to speak. He is offended by it, or, more correctly, he takes it as an occasion to be offended at all existence; he defiantly wills to be himself, to be himself not in spite of it or without it (that would indeed be to abstract himself from it, and that he cannot do, or that would be movement in the direction of resignation)—no, in spite of or in defiance of all existence, he wills to be himself with it, takes it along, almost flouting his agony. Hope in the possibility of help, especially by virtue of the absurd, that for God everything is possible—no, that he does not want. And to seek help from someone else—no, not for all the world does he want that. Rather than to seek help, he prefers, if necessary, to be himself with all the agonies of hell.

That popular notion that "of course, a person who suffers wants to be helped if only someone is able to help him" is not really so, is far from true, even though the contrary instance is not always as deep in despair as the one above. This is how things go. A sufferer usually has one or several ways in which he might want to be helped. If he is helped in these ways, then he is glad to be helped. But when having to be helped becomes a profoundly earnest matter, especially when it means being helped by a superior, or by the supreme one, there is the humiliation of being obliged to accept any kind of help unconditionally, of becoming a nothing in the hand of the "Helper" for whom all things are possible, or the humiliation of simply having to yield to another person, of giving up being himself as long as he is seeking help. Yet there is undoubtedly much suffering, even prolonged and agonized suffering, in which the self nevertheless is not pained in this way, and therefore it fundamentally prefers the suffering along with the retention of being itself.[71]

The more consciousness there is in such a sufferer who in despair wills to be himself, the more his despair intensifies and

---

the admission that it is part of the self, that is, the self will not in faith humble itself under it. Resignation viewed as despair is thus essentially different from the despair of not willing in despair to be oneself, for in despair one does will to be oneself, but with the exclusion of something specific in regard to which one in despair does not will to be oneself.

becomes demonic. It usually originates as follows. A self that in despair wills to be itself is pained in some distress or other that does not allow itself to be taken away from or separated from his concrete self. So now he makes precisely this torment the object of all his passion, and finally it becomes a demonic rage. By now, even if God in heaven and all the angels offered to help him out of it—no, he does not want that, now it is too late. Once he would gladly have given everything to be rid of this agony, but he was kept waiting; now it is too late, now he would rather rage against everything and be the wronged victim of the whole world and of all life, and it is of particular significance to him to make sure that he has his torment on hand and that no one takes it away from him—for then he would not be able to demonstrate and prove to himself that he is right. This eventually becomes such a fixation that for an extremely strange reason he is afraid of eternity, afraid that it will separate him from his, demonically understood, infinite superiority over other men, his justification, demonically understood, for being what he is. —Himself is what he wills to be. He began with the infinite abstraction of the self, and now he has finally become so concrete that it would be impossible to become eternal in that sense; nevertheless, he wills in despair to be himself. What demonic madness—the thought that most infuriates him is that eternity could get the notion to deprive him of his misery.

This kind of despair is rarely seen in the world; such characters really appear only in the poets, the real ones, who always lend "demonic" ideality—using the word in its purely Greek sense—to their creations. Nevertheless, at times despair like this does appear in actuality. What, then, is the corresponding externality? Well, there is nothing "corresponding," inasmuch as a corresponding externality—corresponding to inclosing reserve—is a self-contradiction, for if it corresponds, then it does in fact disclose. But externality in this case is of no consequence whatsoever here where inclosing reserve, or what could be called an inwardness with a jammed lock, must be the particular object of attention. The lowest forms of despair—in which there is really no inwardness, or in any case none worth mentioning—the lowest forms may be presented by describing or discussing some external aspect of the person in despair. But the more spiritual the despair becomes and the more the inwardness becomes a peculiar world of its own in inclosing reserve, the more inconsequential are the externalities under which the despair conceals itself. But the more spiritual despair becomes, the more attention it pays with demonic cleverness to keeping despair closed up in inclosing reserve, and the more attention it pays to neutralizing the externalities, making them as insignificant and inconsequential as possible. Just as the troll in the fairy story disappears through a crevice that no one can see,[72] so it is with despair: the more spiritual it is, the more urgent it is to dwell in an externality behind which no one would ordinarily think of looking for it. This secrecy is itself something spiritual and is one of the safeguards to ensure having, as it were, an *in*-closure [*Indelukke*] behind actuality, a world *ex*-clusively [*udelukkende*] for itself, a world where the self in despair is restlessly and tormentedly engaged in willing to be itself.

XI
184

We began in α(1) with the lowest form of despair: in despair not to will to be oneself.[73] Demonic despair is the most intensive form of the despair: in despair to will to be oneself. It is not even in stoic self-infatuation and self-apotheosis that this despair wills to be itself; it does not will to be itself as that does which, mendaciously to be sure, yet in a certain sense, wills it according to its perfection. No, in hatred toward existence, it wills to be itself, wills to be itself in accordance with its misery. Not even in defiance or defiantly does it will to be itself, but for spite; not even in defiance does it want to tear itself loose from the power that established it, but for spite wants to force itself upon it, to obtrude defiantly upon it, wants to adhere to it out of malice—and, of course, a spiteful denunciation must above all take care to adhere to what it denounces. Rebelling against all existence, it feels that it has obtained evidence against it, against its goodness. The person in despair believes that he himself is the evidence, and that is what he wants to be, and therefore he wants to be himself, himself in his torment, in order to protest against all existence with this torment. Just as the weak, despairing person is unwilling to hear anything about any consolation eternity has for him, so a person in such despair does not want to hear anything about it, either, but for a different reason: this very consolation would be his undoing—as a denunciation of all existence. Figuratively speaking, it is as if an error slipped into an author's writing and the error became conscious of itself as an error—perhaps it actually was not a mistake but in a much higher sense an essential part of the whole production—and now this error wants to mutiny against the author, out of hatred toward him, forbidding him to correct it and in maniacal defiance saying to him: No, I refuse to be erased; I will stand as a witness against you, a witness that you are a second-rate author.

XI
185

Part Two

DESPAIR IS SIN

A[1]

Despair Is Sin

Sin is: *before God, or with the conception of God, in despair not to will to be oneself, or in despair to will to be oneself.* Thus sin is intensified weakness or intensified defiance: sin is the intensification of despair. The emphasis is on *before God*, or with a conception of God; it is the conception of God that makes sin dialectically, ethically, and religiously what lawyers call "aggravated" despair.

Although there is no room or place for a psychological delineation in this part, least of all in section A, reference may be made at this point to the most dialectical frontier between despair and sin, to what could be called a poet-existence[2] verging on the religious, an existence that has something in common with the despair of resignation, except that the concept of God is present. Such a poet-existence, as is discernible in the position and conjunction of the categories, will be the most eminent poet-existence. Christianly understood, every poet-existence (esthetics notwithstanding) is sin, the sin of poetizing instead of being, of relating to the good and the true through the imagination instead of being that—that is, existentially striving to be that. The poet-existence under consideration here is different from despair in that it does have a conception of God or is before God, but it is exceedingly dialectical and is as if in an impenetrable dialectical labyrinth concerning the extent to which it is obscurely conscious of being sin. A poet like that can have a very profound religious longing, and the conception of God is taken up into his despair.
He loves God above all, God who is his only consolation in his secret anguish, and yet he loves the anguish and will not give it up.[3] He would like so very much to be himself before God, but with the exclusion of the fixed point where the self suffers; there in despair he does not will to be himself.

He hopes that eternity will take it away, and here in time, no matter how much he suffers under it, he cannot resolve to take it upon himself, cannot humble himself under it in faith. And yet he continues in the God-relationship, and this is his only salvation; it would be sheer horror for him to have to be without God, "it would be enough to despair over," and yet he actually allows himself—perhaps unconsciously—to poetize God as somewhat different from what God is, a bit more like the fond father who indulges his child's every wish far too much. He becomes a poet of the religious in the same way as one who became a poet through an unhappy love affair and blissfully celebrates the happiness of erotic love. He became unhappy in the religious life, dimly understands that he is required to give up this anguish—that is, in faith to humble himself under it and take it upon himself as a part of the self—for he wants to keep it apart from himself, and precisely in this way he holds on to it, although he no doubt believes this is supposed to result in parting from it as far as possible, giving it up to the greatest extent humanly possible (this, like every word from a person in despair, is inversely correct and consequently to be understood inversely). But in faith to take it upon himself—that he cannot do, that is, in essence he is unwilling or here his self ends in vagueness. Yet this poet's description of the religious—just like that other poet's description of erotic love—has a charm, a lyrical verve that no married man's and no His Reverence's presentations have. Nor is what he says untrue, by no means; his presentation is simply his happier, his better *I*. His relation to the religious is that of an unhappy lover, not in the strictest sense that of a believer; he has only the first element of faith—despair—and within it an intense longing for the religious. His conflict actually is this: Has he been called? Does his thorn in the flesh signify that he is to be used for the extraordinary? Before God, is it entirely in order to be the extraordinary he has become? Or is the thorn in the flesh that under which he must humble himself in order to attain the universally human? —But enough of this. With the accent of truth I may ask: To whom am I speaking? Who cares about these high-powered psychological investigations to the nth degree? The Nürnberg pictures that the pastor paints are better understood; they deceivingly resemble one and all, what most people are, and spiritually understood—nothing.

CHAPTER 1.
THE GRADATIONS IN THE CONSCIOUSNESS OF THE SELF
(THE QUALIFICATION: "BEFORE GOD")⁴

The preceding section concentrated on pointing out a gradation in the consciousness of the self; first came ignorance of having an eternal self (C, B, a), then a knowledge of having a self in which there is something eternal (C, B, b), and under this, in turn (α 1-2, β), gradations were pointed out. This whole deliberation must now dialectically take a new direction. The point is that the previously considered gradation in the consciousness of the self is within the category of the human self, or the self whose criterion is man. But this self takes on a new quality and qualification by being a self directly before God. This self is no longer the merely human self but is what I, hoping not to be misinterpreted, would call the theological self, the self directly before God. And what infinite reality [*Realitet*]⁵ the self gains by being conscious of existing before God, by becoming a human self whose criterion is God! A cattleman who (if this were possible) is a self directly before his cattle is a very low self, and, similarly, a master who is a self directly before his slaves is actually no self—for in both cases a criterion is lacking. The child who previously has had only his parents as a criterion becomes a self as an adult by getting the state as a criterion, but what an infinite accent falls on the self by having God as the criterion! The criterion for the self is always: that directly before which it is a self, but this in turn is the definition of "criterion." Just as only entities of the same kind can be added, so everything is qualitatively that by which it is measured, and that which is its qualitative criterion [*Maalestok*] is ethically its goal [*Maal*]; the criterion and goal are what define something, what it is, with the exception of the condition in the world of freedom, where by not qualitatively being that which is his goal and his criterion a person must himself have merited this disqualification. Thus the goal and the criterion still remain discriminatingly the same, making it clear just what a person is not—namely, that which is his goal and criterion.

It was a very sound idea, one that came up so frequently in an older dogmatics,[6] whereas a later dogmatics[7] very frequently took exception to it because it did not have the understanding or the feeling for it—it was a very sound idea, even if at times it was misapplied: the idea that what makes sin so terrible is that it is before God. It was used to prove eternal punishment in hell. Later, as men became more shrewd, they said: Sin is sin; sin is no greater because it is against God or before God. Strange! Even lawyers speak of aggravated crimes; even lawyers make a distinction between a crime committed against a public official, for example, or against a private citizen, make a distinction between the punishment for a patricide and that for an ordinary murder.

No, the older dogmatics was right in maintaining that because sin is against God it is infinitely magnified. The error consisted in considering God as some externality and in seeming to assume that only occasionally did one sin against God. But God is not some externality in the sense that a policeman is. The point that must be observed is that the self has a conception of God and yet does not will as he wills, and thus is disobedient. Nor does one only occasionally sin before God, for every sin is before God, or, more correctly, what really makes human guilt into sin is that the guilty one has the consciousness of existing before God.

Despair is intensified in relation to the consciousness of the self, but the self is intensified in relation to the criterion for the self, infinitely when God is the criterion. In fact, the greater the conception of God, the more self there is; the more self, the greater the conception of God. Not until a self as this specific single individual is conscious of existing before God, not until then is it the infinite self, and this self sins before God. Thus, despite everything that can be said about it, the selfishness of paganism was not nearly so aggravated as is that of Christendom, inasmuch as there is selfishness here also, for the pagan did not have his self directly before God. The pagan and the natural man have the merely human self as their criterion. Therefore, from a higher point of view, it may be correct to regard paganism as immersed in sin, but the sin of paganism was essentially despairing ignorance of God, of existing before God; paganism is "to be without God in the world."⁸ Therefore, from another point of view, it is true that in the strictest sense the pagan did not sin, for he did not sin before God, and all sin is before God. Furthermore, in one sense it is also quite true that frequently a pagan is assisted in slipping blamelessly through the world simply because he is saved by his superficial Pelagian conception; but then his sin is something else, namely, his superficial Pelagian interpretation.⁹ On the other hand, it is certainly also the case that many a time, precisely by being strictly brought up in Christianity, a person has in a certain sense been plunged into sin because the whole Christian viewpoint was too earnest for him, especially in the early part of his life; but then again there is some help to him in this more profound conception of what sin is.

Sin is: before God in despair not to will to be oneself, or before God in despair to will to be oneself. Even though this definition may in other respects be conceded to have its merits (and of all of them, the most important is that it is the only Scriptural definition, for Scripture always defines sin as disobedience), is not this definition too spiritual? The first and foremost answer to that must be: A definition of sin can never be too spiritual (unless it becomes so spiritual that it abolishes sin), for sin is specifically a qualification of spirit. Furthermore, why is it assumed to be too spiritual? Because it does not mention murder, stealing, fornication, etc.? But does it not speak of these things? Are not they also self-willfulness against God, a disobedience that defies his commandments? On the other hand, if in considering sin we mention only such sins, we so easily forget that, humanly speaking, all such things may be quite in order up to a point, and yet one's

XI
193

whole life may be sin, the familiar kind of sin: the glittering vices,[10] the self-willfulness that either in spiritlessness or with effrontery goes on being or wants to be ignorant of the human self's far, far deeper obligation in obedience to God with regard to its every clandestine desire and thought, with regard to its readiness to hear and understand and its willingness to follow every least hint from God as to his will for this self.[11] The sins of the flesh are the self-willfulness of the lower self, but how often is not one devil driven out with the devil's help and the last condition becomes worse than the first.[12] For this is how things go in the world: first a man sins out of frailty and weakness, and then—well, then he may learn to flee to God and be helped to faith, which saves from all sin, but this will not be discussed here—then he despairs over his weakness and becomes either a pharisee who in despair manages a sort of legal righteousness, or in despair he plunges into sin again.

Therefore, the definition embraces every imaginable and every actual form of sin; indeed, it rightly stresses the crucial point that sin is despair (for sin is not the turbulence of flesh and blood but is the spirit's consent to it) and is: before God. As a definition it is algebra;[13] for me to begin to describe particular sins in this little book would be out of place, and, furthermore, the attempt might fail. The main point here is simply that the definition, like a net, embraces all forms. And this it does, as can be seen if it is tested by posing its opposite: faith, by which I steer in this whole book as by a trustworthy navigation guide. Faith is: that the self in being itself and in willing to be itself rests transparently in God.

Very often, however, it is overlooked that the opposite of sin is by no means virtue. In part, this is a pagan view, which is satisfied with a merely human criterion and simply does not know what sin is, that all sin is before God. No, *the opposite of sin is faith*,[14] as it says in Romans 14:23: "whatever does not proceed from faith is sin." And this is one of the most decisive definitions for all Christianity—that the opposite of sin is not virtue but faith.

Appendix. *That the Definition of Sin Includes*   XI
194
the Possibility of Offense,
a General Observation about Offense

The antithesis sin/faith is the Christian one that Christianly
reshapes all ethical concepts and gives them one additional
range. At the root of the antithesis lies the crucial Christian   XI
195
qualification: before God, a qualification that in turn has
Christianity's crucial criterion: *the absurd, the paradox, the possibility of offense.*[15] That this is demonstrated by every determination of what is Christian is extremely important, because
offense is Christianity's weapon against all speculation. In
what, then, lies the possibility of offense here? It lies in this,
that a human being should have this reality [*Realitet*]: that as
an *individual* human being a person is directly before God and
consequently, as a corollary, that a person's sin should be of
concern to God. The idea of the individual human being—
before God—never enters speculation's mind. It only univer-
salizes individual human beings fantastically into the race.
That, in fact, was also the reason a disbelieving Christianity
made out that sin is sin and that whether it is directly before
God or not makes no difference at all. In other words, it
wanted to get rid of the qualification *before God* and therefore
worked out a higher wisdom that, curiously enough, however, was neither more nor less than what higher wisdom
most often is: the old paganism.

There is so much talk about being offended by Christianity
because it is so dark and gloomy, offended because it is so
rigorous etc., but it would be best of all to explain for once
that the real reason that men are offended by Christianity is
that it is too high, because its goal is not man's goal, because it
wants to make man into something so extraordinary that he
cannot grasp the thought. A very simple psychological exposition of the nature of offense will also explain and show how
very foolishly we have conducted ourselves in defending
Christianity in such a way that the offense has been removed,
how in stupidity or with effrontery we have ignored Christ's

own instructions, which frequently and so concernedly caution against offense;[16] that is, he personally points out that the possibility of offense is there and must be there, for if it is not supposed to be there, if it is not an eternal, essential component of Christianity, then it certainly is so much human nonsense on the part of Christ to be concerned and to go around cautioning against it instead of removing it.

If I were to imagine a poor day laborer and the mightiest emperor who ever lived, and if this mightiest emperor suddenly seized on the idea of sending for the day laborer, who had never dreamed and "in whose heart it had never arisen"[17] that the emperor knew he existed, who then would consider

himself indescribably favored just to be permitted to see the emperor once, something he would relate to his children and grandchildren as the most important event in his life—if the emperor sent for him and told him that he wanted him for a son-in-law: what then? Quite humanly, the day laborer would be more or less puzzled, self-conscious, and embarrassed by it; he would (and this is the humanness of it) humanly find it very strange and bizarre, something he would not dare tell to anyone, since he himself had already secretly concluded what his neighbors near and far would busily gossip about as soon as possible: that the emperor wanted to make a fool of him, make him a laughingstock of the whole city, that there would be cartoons of him in the newspapers, and that the story of his engagement to the emperor's daughter would be sold by the ballad peddlers. This plan for him to become the emperor's son-in-law simply would have to take on an external reality very soon so that the day laborer could be certain in some substantial way of whether the emperor was indeed in earnest about this, or whether he only wanted to pull the poor man's leg, make him unhappy for his whole life, and ultimately send him to a madhouse; for present here is the *quid nimis* [excess] that can so very easily turn into its opposite. A little favor—that would make sense to the laborer. It would be understood in the market town by the esteemed, cultured public, by the ballad peddlers, in short, by the 5 x 100,000 people who lived in that market town,[18] which, to be sure, with respect to population, was even a very large city, but a very small one with respect to having an understanding of and sense for the extraordinary. But this, this plan for him to become a son-in-law, well, that was far too much. Now suppose, however, that the plan dealt not with an external reality but an internal one, so that facticity could not provide the laborer with certainty but that faith itself was the only facticity, and thus everything was left up to faith, whether he had sufficient humble courage to dare to believe it (for brash courage cannot help unto *faith*). How many day laborers are there who would have this courage? The person lacking this courage would be offended; to him the extraordinary would sound like a gibe at him. He would then perhaps honestly and forthrightly confess: Such a thing is too high for me, I cannot grasp it; to be perfectly blunt, to me it is a piece of folly.

And now, what of Christianity! Christianity teaches that this individual human being—and thus every single individual human being, no matter whether man, woman, servant girl, cabinet minister, merchant, barber, student, or whatever—this individual human being exists *before God*, this individual human being who perhaps would be proud of having spoken with the king once in his life, this human being who does not have the slightest illusion of being on intimate terms with this one or that one, this human being exists before God, may speak with God any time he wants to, assured of being heard by him—in short, this person is invited to live on the most intimate terms with God! Furthermore, for this person's sake, also for this very person's sake, God comes to the world, allows himself to be born, to suffer, to die, and this suffering God—he almost implores and beseeches this person to accept the help that is offered to him! Truly, if there is anything to lose one's mind over, this is it! Everyone lacking the humble courage to dare to believe this is offended. But why is he offended? Because it is too high for him, because his mind cannot grasp it, because he cannot attain bold confidence in the

XI
197

face of it and therefore must get rid of it, pass it off as a bagatelle, nonsense, and folly, for it seems as if it would choke him.

For what is offense? Offense is unhappy admiration. Thus it is related to envy, but it is an envy that turns against the person himself, is worse against oneself to an even higher degree. The uncharitableness of the natural man cannot allow him the extraordinary that God has intended for him; so he is offended.

The degree of offense depends on how passionate a man's admiration is. The more prosaic people, lacking in imagination and passion and thus not particularly given to admiration, are also offended, but they limit themselves to saying: Such a thing I just can't understand; I leave it alone. They are the skeptics. But the more passion and imagination a person has—consequently, the closer he is in a certain sense (in possibility) to being able to believe, N.B., to humbling himself in adoration under the extraordinary—the more passionate is his offense, which finally cannot be satisfied with anything less than getting this rooted out, annihilated, trampled into the dirt.

To understand offense, it is necessary to study human envy,[19] an area that I present beyond the examination requirements and fancy myself to have studied thoroughly. Envy is secret admiration. An admirer who feels that he cannot become happy by abandoning himself to it chooses to be envious of that which he admires. So he speaks another language wherein that which he actually admires is a trifle, a rather stupid, insipid, peculiar, and exaggerated thing. Admiration is happy self-surrender; envy is unhappy self-assertion.

It is the same with offense,[20] for that which between man and man is admiration/envy is adoration/offense in the relationship between God and men. The *summa summarum* [sum total] of all human wisdom is this "golden" (perhaps it is more correct to say "plated") mean:[21] *ne quid nimis* [nothing too much]. Too little and too much spoil everything. This is bandied about among men as wisdom, is honored with admiration; its exchange rate never fluctuates, and all mankind

XI
198

guarantees its worth. Now and then there is a genius who goes a little way beyond this, and he is called crazy—by sensible people. But Christianity makes an enormous giant stride beyond this *ne quid nimis* into the absurd; that is where Christianity begins—and offense.

Now we see how extraordinarily stupid (so that there can still be a remnant of something extraordinary) it is to defend Christianity, how little knowledge of human nature it manifests, how it connives even if unconsciously, with offense by making Christianity out to be some poor, miserable thing that in the end has to be rescued by a champion. Therefore, it is certain and true that the first one to come up with the idea of defending Christianity in Christendom is *de facto* a Judas No. 2: he, too, betrays with a kiss,[22] except that his treason is the treason of stupidity. To defend something is always to disparage it. Suppose that someone has a warehouse full of gold, and suppose he is willing to give every ducat to the poor—but in addition, suppose he is stupid enough to begin this charitable enterprise of his with a defense in which he justifies it on three grounds: people will almost come to doubt that he is doing any good. As for Christianity! Well, he who defends it has never believed it. If he believes, then the enthusiasm of faith is not a defense— no, it is attack and victory; a believer is a victor.

So also with Christianity and offense. The possibility of offense is very appropriately present in the Christian definition of sin. It is this: before God. A pagan, the natural man, is very willing to admit that sin exists, but this "before God" that actually makes sin into sin, this is too much for him. For him (although in a way different from that pointed out here) it makes much too much of being human; make it a little less, and he is willing to go along with it—"but too much is too much."

XI
199

CHAPTER 2.
THE SOCRATIC DEFINITION OF SIN

XI
199

Sin is ignorance.[23] This, as is well known, is the Socratic definition, which, like everything Socratic, is an authority meriting attention. But with regard to this point, as with so much that is Socratic, men have come to feel an urge to go further. What countless numbers have felt the urge to go further than Socratic ignorance—presumably because they felt it was impossible for them to stop with that—for how many are there in any generation who could persevere, even for just one month, in existentially expressing ignorance about everything.

By no means, therefore, shall I dismiss the Socratic definition on the grounds that one cannot stop there, but with Christianity *in mente* [in mind], I shall use this Socratic definition to bring out the latter in its radicality—simply because the Socratic definition is so genuinely Greek. And here, as always with any other definition that in the most rigorous sense is not rigorously Christian—that is, every intermediate definition—its emptiness becomes apparent.

The defect in the Socratic definition is its ambiguity as to how the ignorance itself is to be more definitely understood, its origin etc. In other words, even if sin is ignorance (or what Christianity perhaps would rather call stupidity), which in one sense certainly cannot be denied—is this an original ignorance, is it therefore the state of someone who has not known and up until now has not been capable of knowing anything about truth, or is it a resultant, a later ignorance? If it is the latter, then sin must essentially lodge somewhere else than in ignorance. It must lodge in a person's efforts to obscure his knowing. Given this assumption, however, that obstinate and very tenacious ambiguity comes up again: the question of whether a person was clearly aware of his action when he started to obscure his knowing. If he was not clearly aware of it, then his knowing was already somewhat obscured before he began doing it, and the question simply arises again and again. If, however, it is assumed that he was clearly aware of what he was doing when he began to obscure his knowing, then the sin (even if it is ignorance, insofar as this is the result) is not in the knowing but in the willing, and the inevitable question concerns the relation of knowing and

XI
200

willing to each other. With all such matters (and the questioning could go on for days), the Socratic definition really does not concern itself. Socrates was indeed an ethicist, the first (in fact, the founder of ethics, as antiquity unconditionally claims), just as he is and remains the first of his kind, but he begins with ignorance. Intellectually, he tends toward ignorance, toward knowing nothing. Ethically, he interprets ignorance as something quite different and begins with that. On the other hand, Socrates naturally is not an essentially religious ethicist, even less a Christian dogmatician. Therefore, he does not really enter into the whole investigation with which Christianity begins, into the *prius* [antecedent state] in which sin presupposes itself and which is explained in Christianity in the dogma of hereditary sin, the border of which this discussion will merely approach.

Therefore, Socrates does not actually arrive at the category of sin, which certainly is dubious for a definition of sin. How can this be? If sin is ignorance, then sin really does not exist, for sin is indeed consciousness. If sin is being ignorant of what is right and therefore doing wrong, then sin does not exist. If this is sin, then along with Socrates it is assumed that there is no such thing as a person's knowing what is right and doing wrong, or knowing that something is wrong and going ahead and doing wrong. Consequently, if the Socratic definition is sound, then there is no sin at all. Note that, Christianly, this is quite in order, in a deeper sense altogether correct; in the interest of Christianity it is *quod erat demonstrandum* [that which was to be demonstrated]. It is specifically the concept of sin, the teaching about sin, that most decisively differentiates Christianity qualitatively from paganism, and this is also why Christianity very consistently assumes that neither paganism nor the natural man knows what sin is; in fact, it assumes that there has to be a revelation from God to show what sin is. The qualitative distinction between paganism and Christianity is not, as a superficial consideration assumes, the doctrine of the Atonement. No, the beginning must start far deeper, with sin, with the doctrine of sin—as Christianity in fact does. What a

XI
201

dangerous objection it would be against Christianity if paganism had a definition of sin that Christianity would have to acknowledge as correct.

What constituent, then, does Socrates lack for the defining of sin? It is the will, defiance. The intellectuality of the Greeks was too happy, too naive, too esthetic, too ironic, too witty—too sinful—to grasp that anyone could knowingly not do the good, or knowingly, knowing what is right, do wrong. The Greek mind posits an intellectual categorical imperative.[24]

The truth of this should not be disregarded, and it is undoubtedly necessary to underscore it in a time like this, which is running wild in its profusion of empty, pompous, and fruitless knowledge, to the point where now, just as in Socrates' time, only even more so, it is necessary for men to be Socratically starved a little. It is tragic-comic, all these declarations about having understood and grasped the highest, plus the virtuosity with which many *in abstracto* know how to expound it, in a certain sense quite correctly—it is tragic-comic to see that all this knowledge and understanding exercises no power at all over men's lives, that their lives do not express in the remotest way what they have understood, but rather the opposite. On seeing this tragic-comic discrepancy, one involuntarily exclaims: But how in the world is it possible that they could have understood it? Can it be true that they have understood it? At this point, that old ironist and ethicist replies: Don't ever believe it, my friend; they have not understood it, for if they had in truth understood it, their lives would have expressed it also, then they would have done what they had understood.

Does this mean, then, that to understand and to understand are two different things? They certainly are, and the person who has understood this—but, please note, not in the sense of the first kind of understanding—is *eo ipso* initiated into all the secrets of irony. To regard as comic someone who is actually ignorant of something is a very low form of the comic and is unworthy of irony. That men once lived who thought the earth stands still—and they did not know any better—has nothing particularly comic about it. Our age will probably look the same to an age having more knowledge about the physical world. The contrast is between two different ages; a deeper point of coincidence is lacking, but such a contrast is not an essential one and thus is not essentially comic, either. No, but when a man stands and says the right thing, and consequently has understood it, and then when he acts he does the wrong thing, and thus shows that he has not understood it—yes, this is exceedingly comic. It is exceedingly comic that a man, stirred to tears so that not only sweat but also tears pour down his face, can sit and read or hear an exposition on self-denial, on the nobility of sacrificing his life for the truth—and then in the next moment, *ein, zwei, drei, vupti,* almost with tears still in his eyes, be in full swing, in the sweat of his brow and to the best of his modest ability, helping untruth to be victorious. It is exceedingly comic that a speaker with sincere voice and gestures, deeply stirred and deeply stirring, can movingly depict the truth, can face all the powers of evil and of hell boldly, with cool self-assurance in his bearing, a dauntlessness in his air, and an appropriateness of movement worthy of admiration—it is exceedingly comic that almost simultaneously, practically still "in his dressing gown,"[25] he can timidly and cravenly cut and run away from the slightest inconvenience. It is exceedingly comic that someone is able to understand the whole truth about how mean and sordid the world is etc.—that he can understand this and then the next moment not recognize what he has understood, for almost at once he himself goes out and participates in the very same meanness and sordidness, is honored for it, and accepts the honor, that is, acknowledges it. When I see someone[26] who declares he has completely understood how Christ went around in the form of a lowly servant,[27] poor, despised, mocked, and, as Scripture tells us, spat upon[28]— when I see the same person assiduously make his way to the place where in worldly sagacity it is good to be,[29] set himself up as securely as possible, when I see him then so anxiously, as if his life depended on it, avoiding every gust of unfavorable wind from the right or the left, see him so blissful, so extremely blissful, so slap-happy, yes, to make it complete, so slap-happy that he even thanks God for—for being whole-heartedly honored and esteemed by all, by everyone—then I have often said privately to myself: "Socrates, Socrates, Socrates, can it be possible that this man has understood what he says he has understood?" This is how I talked—indeed, I have also wished that Socrates was right, for it seems to me as if Christianity were too rigorous, and in accordance with my own experience I cannot make such a person out to be a hypocrite. No, Socrates, you I can understand; you make him into a joker, a jolly fellow of sorts, and fair game for laughter; you have nothing against but rather even approve of my preparing and serving him up as something comic—provided I do it well.

Socrates, Socrates, Socrates! Yes, we may well call your name three times; it would not be too much to call it ten times, if it would be of any help. Popular opinion maintains that the world needs a republic, needs a new social order and a new religion—but no one considers that what the world, confused simply by too much knowledge, needs is a Socrates. Of course, if anyone thought of it, not to mention if many thought of it, he would be less needed. Invariably, what error needs most is always the last thing it thinks of—quite natural-ly, for otherwise it would not, after all, be error.

So it could very well be that our age needs an ironic-ethical correction such as this—this may actually be the only thing it needs—for obviously it is the last thing it thinks of. Instead of going beyond Socrates, it is extremely urgent that we come back to this Socratic principle—to understand and to under-stand are two things—not as a conclusion that ultimately as-sists men in their deepest misery, since that annuls precisely the difference between understanding and understanding, but as the ethical conception of everyday life.

The Socratic definition works out in the following way. When someone does not do what is right, then neither has he understood what is right. His understanding is purely imagi-nary; his declaration of having understood is false informa-tion; his repeated protestation that he will be hanged if he has

not understood puts him far, far along on the most roundabout way. But then the definition is indeed correct. If someone does the right thing, then he certainly does not sin; and if
he does not do what is right, then he did not understand it,
either; if he had really and truly understood it, it would
quickly have prompted him to do it, it would quickly have
made him a Chladni figure for his understanding: ergo, sin is
ignorance.

But wherein is the definition defective? Its defect is something the Socratic principle itself realizes and remedies, but
only to a certain degree: it lacks a dialectical determinant appropriate to the transition from having understood something
to doing it. In this transition Christianity begins; by taking
this path, it shows that sin is rooted in willing and arrives at
the concept of defiance, and then, to fasten the end[30] very
firmly, it adds the doctrine of hereditary sin[31]—alas, for
speculation's secret in comprehending is simply to sew without fastening the end and without knotting the thread, and
this is why, wonder of wonders, it can go on sewing and sewing, that is, pulling the thread through. Christianity, on the
other hand, fastens the end by means of the paradox.

In pure ideality, where the actual individual person is not
involved, the transition is necessary (after all, in the system[32]
everything takes place of necessity), or there is no difficulty at
all connected with the transition from understanding to doing. This is the Greek mind (but not the Socratic, for Socrates
is too much of an ethicist for that). And the secret of modern
philosophy is essentially the very same, for it is this: *cogito ergo
sum* [I think therefore I am],[33] to think is to be (Christianly,
however, it reads: according to your faith, be it unto you, or,
as you believe, so you are, to believe is to be[34]). Thus it is evi-
dent that modern philosophy is neither more nor less than
paganism. But this is not the worst possible situation—to be
in kinship with Socrates is not too bad. But the totally un-
Socratic aspect of modern philosophy is that it wants to de-
lude us into believing that this is Christianity.

In the world of actuality, however, where the individual
person is involved, there is this tiny little transition from hav-

ing understood to doing; it is not always quick, *cito citissime* [very quick], it is not (if I, lacking philosophical language, may speak German) *geschwind wie der Wind* [fast as the wind]. Quite the opposite, this is the beginning of a very long-winded story.

In the life of the spirit there is no standing still [*Stilstand*] (really no state [*Tilstand*], either; everything is actuation); therefore, if a person does not do what is right at the very second he knows it—then, first of all, knowing simmers down. Next comes the question of how willing appraises what is known. Willing is dialectical and has under it the entire lower nature of man. If willing does not agree with what is known, then it does not necessarily follow that willing goes ahead and does the opposite of what knowing understood (presumably such strong opposites are rare); rather, willing allows some time to elapse, an interim called: "We shall look at it tomorrow." During all this, knowing becomes more and more obscure, and the lower nature gains the upper hand more and more; alas, for the good must be done immediately, as soon as it is known (and that is why in pure ideality the transition from thinking to being is so easy, for there everything is at once), but the lower nature's power lies in stretching things out. Gradually, willing's objection to this development lessens; it almost appears to be in collusion. And when knowing has become duly obscured, knowing and willing can better understand each other; eventually they agree completely, for now knowing has come over to the side of willing and admits that what it wants is absolutely right. And this is how perhaps the great majority of men live: they work gradually at eclipsing their ethical and ethical-religious comprehension, which would lead them out into decisions and conclusions that their lower nature does not much care for, but they expand their esthetic and metaphysical comprehension, which ethically is a diversion.

Nevertheless, with all this we have still gone no further than the Socratic principle, for Socrates would say: If this happens, it just shows that a person such as this still has not understood what is right. This means that the Greek mind does not have the courage to declare that a person knowingly does wrong, knows what is right and does the wrong; so it manages by saying: If a person does what is wrong, he has not understood what is right.

Absolutely right. And no *human being* can come further than that; no man of himself and by himself can declare what sin is, precisely because he is in sin; all his talk about sin is basically a glossing over of sin, an excuse, a sinful watering down. That is why Christianity begins in another way: man has to learn what sin is by a revelation from God;[35] sin is not a matter of a person's not having understood what is right but of his being unwilling to understand it, of his not willing what is right.

XI
206

Socrates actually gives no explanation at all of the distinction: not *being able* to understand and not *willing* to understand; on the other hand, he is the grand master of all ironists in operating by means of the distinction between understanding and understanding. Socrates explains that he who does not do what is right has not understood it, either; but Christianity goes a little further back and says that it is because he is unwilling to understand it, and this again because he does not will what is right. And in the next place it teaches that a person does what is wrong (essentially defiance) even though he understands what is right, or he refrains from doing what is right even though he understands it; in short, the Christian teaching about sin is nothing but offensiveness toward man, charge upon charge; it is the suit that the divine as the prosecutor ventures to bring against man.

But can any human being comprehend this Christian teaching? By no means, for it is indeed Christianity and therefore involves offense. It must be believed. To comprehend is the range of man's relation to the human, but to believe is man's relation to the divine. How then does Christianity explain this incomprehensibility? Very consistently, in a way just as incomprehensible: by revealing it.

Therefore, interpreted Christianly, sin has its roots in willing, not in knowing, and this corruption of willing affects the individual's consciousness. This is entirely consistent, for otherwise the question of the origin of sin would have to be posed in regard to each individual.

Here again is the mark of offense. The possibility of offense lies in this: there must be a revelation from God to teach man what sin is and how deeply it is rooted. The natural man, the pagan, thinks like this: "All right, I admit that I have not understood everything in heaven and on earth. If there has to be a revelation, then let it teach us about heavenly things; but it is most unreasonable that there should be a revelation informing us what sin is. I do not pretend to be perfect, far from it; nevertheless, I do know and I am willing to admit how far from perfect I am. Should I, then, not know what sin is?" But Christianity replies: No, that is what you know least of all, how far from perfect you are and what sin is. —Note that in this sense, looked at from the Christian point of view, sin is indeed ignorance: it is ignorance of what sin is.

Therefore the definition of sin given in the previous section still needs to be completed as follows: sin is—after being taught by a revelation from God what sin is—before God in despair not to will to be oneself or in despair to will to be oneself.

CHAPTER 3.
SIN IS NOT A NEGATION BUT A POSITION[36]

That this is the case is something that orthodox dogmatics and orthodoxy on the whole have always contended, and they have rejected as pantheistic any definition of sin that made it out to be something merely negative—weakness, sensuousness, finitude, ignorance, etc. Orthodoxy has perceived very correctly that the battle must be fought here, or, as in the preceding portion, here the end must be fastened very firmly, here it is a matter of holding back; orthodoxy has correctly perceived that when sin is defined negatively, all Christianity is flabby and spineless. That is why orthodoxy emphasizes that there must be a revelation from God to teach fallen man what sin is, a communication that, quite consistently, must be believed, because it is a dogma.[37] And, of course, paradox, faith, and dogma—these three constituents have an agreement and an alliance that are the surest solidarity and bulwark against all pagan wisdom.

So it is with orthodoxy. Then, through a curious misunderstanding, a so-called speculative dogmatics,[38] which was involved with philosophy in a dubious way, thought it could *comprehend* this qualification that sin is a position. But if this is true, then sin is a negation. The secret of all comprehending is that this comprehending is itself higher than any position it posits; the concept establishes a position, but the comprehension of this is its very negation. Aware of this up to a point, speculative dogmatics has nonetheless known no other recourse than to throw up a detachment of assertions at the point where a movement is being made—which is scarcely fitting in a philosophic science. With mounting solemnity each succeeding time, with ever more swearing and cursing, it is asserted that sin is a position and that to say that sin is merely a negation is pantheism and rationalism and God knows what else, but all of it something that speculative dogmatics renounces and abominates—and then a switch is made to comprehending that sin is a position. In other words, it is position only to some extent, not any more than can be comprehended.

XI
208

This duplicity on the part of speculation shows itself at another yet related point. The category of sin or how sin is defined is crucial for the category of repentance. Since the negation of negation is so speculative, the only possibility is that repentance must be the negation of negation—and thus sin becomes negation. —Incidentally, it would certainly be desirable if at some time a sober thinker would explain to what extent the purely logical, which is reminiscent of logic's first relation to grammar (two negatives affirm) and of mathematics—to what extent the logical has validity in the world of actuality, in the world of qualities, whether on the whole the dialectic of qualities is not something different, whether "transition" does not play another role here. *Sub specie aeterno modo* [under the aspect of eternity, in the mode of eternity][39] etc., there is indeed no spacing out at all; therefore everything *is*, and there simply is no transition. To *posit* in this abstract medium is *eo ipso* the same as to *nullify*. But to look at actuality in the same way borders on madness. *In abstracto* it may also be said: the *Perfectum* [perfect tense] follows the *Imperfectum* [imperfect tense]. But if in the world of actuality a person were to conclude from this that it follows of itself and follows immediately that a work he did not complete (*imperfectum*) was completed, he would certainly be crazy. It is the same with sin's so-called position if the medium wherein it is placed is pure thought; that medium is far too elusive for the position to be taken seriously.

But all these matters do not concern me here. I steadfastly hold to the Christian teaching that sin is a position—yet not as if it could be comprehended, but as a paradox that must be believed. In my opinion this teaching is sound. If all attempts to comprehend can just be shown to be self-contradictory, then the matter will fall into proper perspective, then it will be clear that whether one will believe or not must be left to faith. —I can very well comprehend (and this is by no means too divine to be comprehended) that someone who by all means has to comprehend and can think only of what claims to be comprehensible will find this very meager. But if all Christianity turns on this, that it *must* be believed and not comprehended, that *either* it must be believed *or* one must be scandalized and offended by it—is it then so praiseworthy to want to comprehend? Is it such great merit or is it not rather insolence or thoughtlessness to want to comprehend that which does not want to be comprehended? If a king decides he wants to be completely incognito, to be treated without exception as an ordinary man, is it then right to pay him royal homage because people generally consider it a greater honor to do so? Or is it not in fact an assertion of oneself and one's own thinking over against the king's will if a person does what he himself wants instead of submitting? Or, I wonder, would the king be pleased at the ever greater ingenuity such a person could show in according him the respect of a subject when the king did not wish to be treated that way—indeed, the ever greater ingenuity such a person could show in going against the king's

XI
209

will? —So let others admire and praise him who pretends to be able to comprehend Christianity. I consider it an outright ethical task, perhaps requiring not a little self-denial in these very speculative times, when all "the others" are busy comprehending, to admit that one is neither able nor obliged to comprehend it. Precisely this is no doubt what our age, what Christendom needs: a little Socratic ignorance with respect to Christianity—but please note, a little "Socratic" ignorance. Let us never forget—but how many ever really knew it or thought it—let us never forget that Socrates' ignorance was a kind of fear and worship of God, that his ignorance was the Greek version of the Jewish saying: The fear of the Lord is the beginning of wisdom.[40] Let us never forget that it was out of veneration for God that he was ignorant, that as far as it was possible for a pagan he was on guard duty as a *judge* on the frontier between God and man, keeping watch so that the deep gulf of qualitative difference between them was maintained, between God and man, that God and man did not merge in some way, *philosophice, poetice* [philosophically, poetically], etc., into one. That was why Socrates was the ignorant one, and that was why the deity found him to be the wisest of men.[41] —Christianity teaches that everything essentially Christian depends solely upon faith; therefore it wants to be precisely a Socratic, God-fearing ignorance, which by means of ignorance guards faith against speculation, keeping watch so that the gulf of qualitative difference between God and man[42] may be maintained as it is in the paradox and faith, so that God and man do not, even more dreadfully than ever in paganism, do not merge in some way, *philosophice, poetice*, etc., into one—in the system.

XI
210

That sin is a position can be made clear from only one side. The preceding section on despair constantly pointed out an escalation. This escalation is manifest partly in the intensification of the consciousness of the self and partly in the intensification consisting in moving from being acted upon to conscious action. Both manifestations jointly indicate that despair does not come from the outside but from within. To the same degree it also becomes more and more established as a position. But according to the definition of sin as set forth, the self infinitely intensified by the conception of God is part of sin and is likewise the greatest possible consciousness of sin as an act. —This signifies that sin is a position;[43] that it is *before God* is the definitely positive element in it.

Moreover, the qualification that sin is a position implies in a quite different sense the possibility of offense, the paradox. That is, the paradox is the implicit consequence of the doctrine of the Atonement. First of all, Christianity proceeds to establish sin so firmly as a position that the human understanding can never comprehend it; and then it is this same Christian teaching that again undertakes to eliminate this position in such a way that the human understanding can never comprehend it. Speculation, which talks itself out of the paradoxes, snips off a little bit from both sides and thereby gets along more easily—it does not make sin quite so positive—but nevertheless cannot get it through its head that sin is to be completely forgotten. But Christianity, which was the first to discover the paradoxes, is as paradoxical on this point as possible; it seems to be working against itself by establishing sin so securely as a position that now it seems to be utterly impossible to eliminate it again—and then it is this very Christianity that by means of the Atonement wants to eliminate sin as completely as if it were drowned in the sea.[44]

XI
211

XI
211

APPENDIX TO A

But Then in a Certain Sense
Does Not Sin Become a Great Rarity?
(The Moral)

In Part One it was pointed out that the more intensive despair becomes, the rarer it is in the world. But if sin is now despair qualitatively intensified once again, presumably this despair must be extremely rare. What a strange problem! Christianity regards everything as under sin;[45] we have tried to depict the Christian point of view as rigorously as possible—and then this strange outcome emerges, this strange conclusion that sin is not to be found at all in paganism but only in Judaism and Christendom, and there again very seldom.

Yet this is entirely correct, but in one sense only and in this way. To sin is: "after being taught by a revelation from God what sin is, before God in despair not to will to be oneself or in despair to will to be oneself"[46]—and indeed, seldom is there a person who is so mature, so transparent to himself, that this can apply to him. But what is the result of this? Here one must take great care, for there is a special dialectical turn. The conclusion was not drawn that a person who is not in a more intensive state of despair is therefore not in despair. On the contrary, it was specifically shown that by far the great majority of men are in despair, but to a lesser degree. But there is nothing meritorious about being in despair to a higher degree. Esthetically it is an advantage, for esthetically there is concern only for vigor; but ethically the more intensive form of despair is further from salvation than the lesser form.

It is the same with sin. Most men are characterized by a dialectic of indifference and live a life so far from the good (faith) that it is almost too spiritless to be called sin—indeed, almost too spiritless to be called despair.

It is certainly true that there is no merit in being a sinner in the strictest sense of the word. But, on the other hand, how in the world can an essential sin-consciousness be found in a life that is so immersed in triviality and silly aping of "the others" that it can hardly be called sin, a life that is too spiritless to be called sin and is worthy only, as Scripture says, of being "spewed out."[47]

This does not dispose of the matter, however, for the dialectic of sin simply ensnares in another way. How does it happen that a person's life becomes so spiritless that Christianity seemingly cannot be brought to bear upon it all, just as when a jack (and Christianity's elevating is a jacking up) cannot be used because there is no firm ground but only marsh-

XI
212

land and bog? Is it something that happens to a person? No, it is his own fault. No one is born devoid of spirit, and no matter how many go to their death with this spiritlessness as the one and only outcome of their lives, it is not the fault of life.

Nevertheless, it has to be said, and as frankly as possible, that so-called Christendom (in which all are Christians by the millions as a matter of course, and thus there are just as many—exactly just as many—Christians as there are people) is not merely a shabby edition of the essentially Christian, full of printer's errors that distort the meaning and of thoughtless omissions and admixtures, but is also a misuse of it, a profanation and prostitution of Christianity. In a little country, scarcely three poets are born in any one generation, but there are plenty of clergymen, many more than can obtain appointments. A poet is said to have a call, but in the opinion of most people (consequently of most Christians) passing an examination is sufficient qualification to become a pastor. And yet a true pastor is even more rare than a true poet; indeed, the word "call"[48] originally belonged to the religious life. But in Christendom there is still a remnant of the notion that being a poet is something and that there is something to its being a call. However, in the eyes of most people (consequently of most Christians) being a pastor has been deserted by every elevating conception; it is, *in puris naturalibus* [without circumlocution], a way of making a living, devoid of the slightest mystery. "Call" signifies an official appointment; the expression "to receive a call" is used, but "to have a call"—well, that is used, too, about someone who has a call to give away.[49]

Alas, the fate of this word in Christendom is like an epigram on everything that is essentially Christian. The trouble is not that Christianity is not voiced (thus the trouble is not that there are not enough pastors) but that it is voiced in such a way that the majority eventually think it utterly inconsequential (just as the majority consider being a pastor no different at all from being a merchant, lawyer, bookbinder, veterinarian, etc. on weekdays). Thus the highest and the holiest things make no impact whatsoever, but they are given sound and are listened to as something that now, God knows why, has become routine and habit like so much else. So what wonder is it that they, instead of finding their own personal conduct indefensible, find it necessary to defend Christianity.

A pastor certainly ought to be a believer. A believer! And a believer, after all, is a lover; as a matter of fact, when it comes to enthusiasm, the most rapturous lover of all lovers is but a stripling compared with a believer. Imagine a lover. Is it not true that he would be capable of speaking about his beloved all day long and all night, too, day in and day out? But do you believe it could ever occur to him, do you believe it would be possible for him, do you not think he would find it loathsome to speak in such a manner that he would try to demonstrate by means of three reasons that there is something to being in love—somewhat as the pastor proves by means of three reasons that praying is beneficial, because praying has become so cheap that in order to raise its prestige a little three reasons have to be adduced. Or the way the pastor—and this is the same, only even more ridiculous—proves with three reasons that to pray is a bliss that "passes all understanding." What a priceless anticlimax[50]—that something that passes all understanding—is proved by three reasons, which, if they do anything at all, presumably do not pass all understanding and, quite the contrary, inevitably make it obvious to the understanding that this bliss by no means passes all understanding, for "reasons," after all, lie in the realm of the understanding. No, for that which passes all understanding—and for him who believes in it—three reasons mean no more than three bottles or three deer! —To go on, do you believe that a lover would ever think of conducting a defense of his being in love, that is, admit that to him it was not the absolute, unconditionally the absolute, but that he thought of it as being in a class with arguments against it and on that basis developed a defense; that is, do you believe that he could or would confess that he was not in love, inform against himself that he was not in love? And if someone were to suggest to a lover that he speak this way, do you not believe that the lover would consider him crazy; and if besides being in love he was also some-

thing of an observer, do you not think he would suspect that
the person suggesting this to him had never known what love
is or wanted him to betray and deny his love—by defending
it? —Is it not obvious that the person who is really in love
would never dream of wanting to prove it by three reasons or
to defend it, for he is something that is more than all reasons
and any defense: he is in love. Anyone who does it is not in
love; he merely pretends to be, and unfortunately—or
fortunately—he is so stupid that he merely informs against
himself as not being in love.

But this is just exactly the way they speak about Christianity, these believing pastors; they either "defend" Christianity
or transpose it into "reasons," if they do not go further and
tinker speculatively with "comprehending" it. This is called
preaching, and in Christendom this kind of preaching and the
fact that someone listens to it is even considered to be a great
thing. This is precisely why Christendom (this is the proof of
it) is so far from being what it calls itself that the lives of most
men, Christianly understood, are far too spiritless to be called
sin in the strictly Christian sense.[51]

B

The Continuance of Sin

Every state of sin is a new sin, or, to express it more precisely, as will be done in this next section, the state of sin is the new sin, is the sin. The sinner may consider this an overstatement; at most he acknowledges that each actual new sin is a new sin. But eternity, which keeps his account, must register the state of sin as new sin. It has only two rubrics, and "Whatever does not proceed from faith is sin";[52] every unrepented sin is a new sin and every moment that it remains unrepented is also new sin. But how rare is the person who has continuity with regard to his consciousness of himself! As a rule, men are conscious only momentarily, conscious in the midst of big decisions, but they do not take the daily everyday into account at all; they are spirit of sorts for an hour one day a week—which, of course, is a rather crude way to be spirit. But eternity is the essential continuity and demands this of a person or that he be conscious as spirit and have faith. The sinner, however, is so much in the power of sin that he has no idea of its wholly encompassing nature, that he is lost and on the way to destruction. He takes into account only each particular new sin that seems to give him new impetus on the road to destruction,[53] just as if he were not proceeding along that way the moment before with all the impetus of his previous sins. Sin has become so natural to him, or sin has become so much his second nature, that he finds the daily everyday to be entirely in order, and he himself pauses only for a moment each time he perceives new impetus, so to speak, from new sin. In his lostness, he is blind to the fact that his life has the continuity of sin instead of the essential continuity of the eternal through being before God in faith.

"The continuity of sin"—but is not sin specifically the discontinuous? So here it is again, this view that sin is merely a negation, which like stolen goods can never be legitimized—a negation, a powerless attempt to establish itself, which, however, undergoing all the torment of powerlessness in despairing defiance, it is incapable of doing. Yes, this is how it is speculatively, but Christianly (this must be believed, since it is indeed the paradox that no man can comprehend) sin is a position that on its own develops an increasingly established continuity.

The law for the growth of this continuity is not the same as the law for the increment of a debt or of a negation. For a debt does not grow because it is not paid; it grows every time it is increased. But sin grows every moment that one does not take leave of it. The sinner is so mistaken in regarding only each new sin as an increase in sin that, from the point of view of Christianity, the state of sin is actually greater sin than the new sin. There is even a proverb that says to sin is human but to remain in sin is of the devil; Christianly, however, this proverb surely must have a different interpretation. The cursory observation that merely looks at the new sin and skips what lies between, what lies between the two particular sins, is just as superficial as supposing that a train moves only when the locomotive puffs. No, this puff and the subsequent propulsion are not what should be considered but rather the steady impetus with which the locomotive proceeds and which produces that puffing. And so it is with sin. In the deepest sense, the state of sin is the sin; the particular sins are not the continuance of sin but the expression for the continuance of sin; in the specific new sin the impetus of sin merely becomes more perceptible to the eye.

The state of sin is a worse sin than the particular sins; it is the sin. Understood in this way, the abiding and lingering in sin is the continuance of sin, is the new sin. The common view is different, that the one sin gives birth to new sin. But it has a far deeper root, namely, that the state of sin is new sin. The line Shakespeare gives to Macbeth (III, 2) is psychologically masterful: *Sündentsprossne Werke erlangen nur durch Sünde Kraft und Stärke* [Works arising in sin gain strength and power only through sin].[54] In other words, deep within itself sin has a consistency, and in this consistency in evil itself it also has a certain strength. But such an observation is never arrived at by merely looking at the particular sins.

Most men probably live with all too little consciousness of themselves to have any idea of what consistency is; that is, they do not exist *qua* spirit. Their lives—either in a certain endearing childish naiveté or in shallow triviality—are made up of some action of sorts, some incidents, of this and that: now they do something good, and then something stupid, and then they begin all over again; now they are in despair for an afternoon, perhaps for three weeks, but then they are jolly fellows again, and then once again in despair for a day. They play along in life, so to speak, but they never experience putting everything together on one thing, never achieve the idea of an infinite self-consistency. That is why they are always talking among themselves about the particular, particular good deeds, particular sins.

Every existence that is within the qualification spirit, even if only on its own responsibility and at its own risk, has an essential interior consistency and a consistency in something higher, at least in an idea. Such a person has great fear of any inconsistency, because he has an immense apprehension of what the result can be, that he could be torn out of the totality in which he has his life. The slightest inconsistency is an enormous loss, for, after all, he loses consistency. In that very moment, the spell is perhaps broken, the mysterious power that bound all his capacities in harmony is diminished, the coiled spring is slackened; everything perhaps becomes a chaos in which the capacities in mutiny battle one another and plunge the self into suffering, a chaos in which there is no agreement within itself, no momentum, no *impetus*. The enormous machine that in consistency was so tractable in its steely strength, so supple in all its power, is out of order; and the better, the more imposing the machine was, the more dreadful the tangled confusion. —The believer, one who rests in and has his life in the consistency of the good, has an infinite fear of even the slightest sin, for he faces an infinite loss. Immediate individuals, the childlike or childish, have no totality to lose; they always win and lose only something particular or something in particular.

As it is with the believer in regard to the internal consistency of sin, so also with his opposite, the demonic person. The situation of the demonic person is similar to that of the alcoholic, who keeps himself in a perpetual state of intoxication out of fear of stopping and of the resulting debility and its possible consequences if he were to be completely sober for one day. Indeed, there are examples of exactly the same attitude in a demoniac as in the good man, who, when sin is temptingly pictured to him in some of its alluring forms, implores: "Tempt me not!" Confronted by someone stronger in the good than himself, the demoniac, when the good is described by that one in all its sublimity, can plead for himself, can tearfully plead that that one will not speak to him, that he will not—as he phrases it—make him weak. Precisely because the demonic person has an internal consistency and is consistent in the consistency of evil, he also has a totality to lose. One single moment of inconsistency, one single dietetic imprudence, one single sidelong glance, one moment of looking at and understanding the whole thing or just a part of it in another way—and he perhaps would never be himself again, so he says. In other words, in despair he has abandoned the good; it cannot help him anyway, but it certainly could disturb him, could make it impossible for him ever again to achieve the full momentum of consistency, could make him weak. Only in the continuance of sin is he himself, only in that does he live and have an impression of himself. But what does this mean? It means that the state of sin is what holds him together deep down where he has sunk, profanely strengthening him with its consistency. It is not the particular new sin that assists him (yes, this is dreadfully deranged!); rather, the particular new sin is merely the expression for the state of sin, which is actually the sin.

Therefore "the continuance of sin," which is now to be discussed, does not mean the particular new sins as much as the state of sin, which in turn becomes the internal intensification of sin, a conscious remaining in the state of sin, so that the law of motion in intensification, here as everywhere else, is inward, in greater and greater intensity of consciousness.

A.
THE SIN OF DESPAIRING OVER ONE'S SIN[55]

Sin is despair; the intensification is the new sin of despairing over one's sin. It is obvious, of course, that this is in the category of intensification; it is not a new sin in the manner of one who stole a hundred dollars and steals a thousand the next time. No, we are not talking about particular sins here; the state of sin is the sin, and this is intensified in a new consciousness.

To despair over one's sin indicates that sin has become or wants to be internally consistent. It wants nothing to do with the good, does not want to be so weak as to listen occasionally to other talk. No, it insists on listening only to itself, on having dealings only with itself; it closes itself up within itself, indeed, locks itself inside one more inclosure, and protects itself against every attack or pursuit by the good by despairing over sin. It is aware of having burned the bridge behind it and of thereby being inaccessible to the good and of the good being inaccessible to it, so that if in a weak moment it should itself will the good, that would still be impossible. Sin itself is severance from the good, but despair over sin is the second severance. This, of course, squeezes the uttermost demonic powers out of sin, gives it the profane toughness or perverseness that must consistently regard everything called repentance and grace not only as empty and meaningless but also as its enemy, as something against which a defense must be made most of all, just as the good defends itself against temptation. Interpreted this way, Mephistopheles (in *Faust*)[56] quite properly says that nothing is more miserable than a devil who despairs, for here despair must be interpreted as a willingness to be weak enough to hear something about repentance and grace. To describe the intensification in the relation between sin and despair over sin, the first may be termed the break with the good and the second with repentance.

Despair over sin is an effort to survive by sinking even deeper. Just as a balloonist ascends by throwing off weights, so the person in despair sinks by more and more determinedly throwing off all the good (for the weight of the good is elevating); he sinks, privately thinking, of course, that he is ascending—and he is indeed growing lighter. Sin itself is the struggle of despair; but then, when all the powers are depleted, there may be a new intensification, a new demonic closing up within himself: this is despair over sin. It is a step forward, a heightening of the demonic, and of course an absorption in sin. It is an effort to give stability and interest to sin as a power by deciding once and for all that one will refuse to hear anything about repentance and grace. Nevertheless, despair over sin is conscious particularly of its own emptiness, that it has nothing on which to live, not even an idea of its own self. Macbeth's lines (II, 2) are psychologically masterful: *Von jetzt* (after he has murdered the king—and now despairs over his sin) *giebt es nicht Ernstes mehr im Leben; Alles ist Tand, gestorben Ruhm und Gnade* [For, from this instant, there's nothing serious in mortality; All is but toys, renown and grace is dead].[57] The masterful stroke is the double turn in the last words (r e n o w n and g r a c e [*R u h m und G n a d e*]). By sin, that is, by despairing over his sin, he has lost all relation to grace—and also to himself. His selfish self culminates in ambition. He has now in fact become the king, and yet, in despairing over his sin and of the reality of repentance, of grace, he has also lost himself; he cannot even keep on going by himself, and he is no closer to enjoying his self at the height of his ambition than he is to grasping grace.

In life (insofar as despair over sin is found in life, but in any case there is something that people describe as that) there are frequent misconceptions about this despair over sin, presumably because of a universal preoccupation with frivolity, thoughtlessness, and sheer triviality, and for this reason people as a rule become quite formal and deferentially take off their hats to any manifestation of something deeper. Either in confused haziness about itself and its significance, or with a streak of hypocrisy, or by way of the craftiness and sophistry intrinsic to all despair, despair over sin is not averse to giving itself the appearance of being something good. Then it is supposed to be the mark of a deep nature, which therefore is so sensitive about its sin. For example, if a person who has been addicted to some sin or other but has successfully resisted temptation for a long time has a relapse and again succumbs to temptation, then the depression that sets in is by no means always sorrow over the sin. It can be something very different; for that matter, it may be a bitterness against Governance, as if it were responsible for his succumbing to temptation, as if it ought not to have been so hard on him, since he had successfully resisted temptation for such a long time. In any case, it is altogether effeminate straightway to regard this sorrow as good, not to be in the least aware of the duplicity in all passionateness, which in turn is a sense of the ominous that can make the passionate one understand later, almost to the point of madness, that he has said the very opposite of what he intended to say.[58] Such a person emphatically declares, perhaps in ever stronger terms, that this relapse plagues and torments him, brings him to despair, and he says: "I will never forgive myself." This is supposed to show how much good there is in him, what a deep nature he has. It is a subterfuge. I deliberately used that stock phrase, "I will never forgive myself," words commonly heard in this connection. And with this very phrase one can immediately straighten out oneself dialectically. He will never forgive himself—but now if God would forgive him this, well, he certainly could have the goodness to forgive himself. No, his despair over the sin is a far cry from being a qualification of the good, is a more intensive qualification of sin, the intensity of which is absorption in sin—and it is this most of all when he is passionately repeating this phrase and thereby denouncing himself (the least of his considerations), when he "never will forgive himself" for sinning like that (for this kind of talk is exactly the opposite of the brokenhearted contrition that prays God to forgive). The point is that during the time that he was successfully resisting temptation he appeared in his own eyes to be better than he actually was, he became proud of himself. It is to this pride's advantage that the past be altogether a thing of the past. But in this relapse the past suddenly becomes very much present again. His pride cannot bear this reminder, and that is the reason for his profound distress etc. But the distress clearly indicates a movement away from God, a secret selfishness and pride, and is a substitute for humbly beginning by humbly thanking God that he helped him to resist temptation for so long a time, acknowledging before God and himself that it is already much more than he deserved, and then humbling himself under the recollection of what he has been.

XI
222

Here, as everywhere, is what the old devotional books explain so profoundly, so experientially, so instructively. They teach that God sometimes lets the believer stumble and fall in some temptation or other, precisely in order to humble him and thereby to establish him better in the good; the contrast between the relapse and the possibly significant progress in the good is very humiliating, the identity with himself very painful. The better a person is, the more acutely painful the particular sin naturally is, and the more dangerous is the slightest bit of impatience if he does not make the right turn. In his sorrow, he may sink into the darkest depression—and a fool of a spiritual counselor may be on the verge of admiring his deep soul and the powerful influence good has on him—as if this were of the good. And his wife, well, she feels deeply humbled by comparison with such an earnest and holy man who can sorrow over his sin in this way. His talk may be even more deceptive; he may not say: I can never forgive myself (as if he had previously forgiven himself sins—a blasphemy). No, he says that God can never forgive him for it. Alas, this is just a subterfuge. His sorrow, his cares, his despair are selfish (just like the anxiety about sin, which sometimes practically drives a man anxiously into sin because it is self-love that wants to be proud of itself, to be without sin), and consolation is the least of his needs; therefore the prodigious number of reasons that spiritual counselors prescribe for taking consolation merely makes the sickness worse.

B.

THE SIN OF DESPAIRING OF* THE FORGIVENESS
OF SINS (OFFENSE)

XI
223

At this point the intensification of the consciousness of the self is the knowledge of Christ, a self directly before Christ. First came (in Part One) ignorance of having an eternal self, then knowledge of having a self in which there is something eternal. Then (in the transition to Part Two) it was pointed out that this distinction is included under the self that has a human conception of itself or that has man as the criterion. The counterpart to this was a self directly before God, and this constituted the basis for the definition of sin.

Now a self comes directly before Christ, a self that in despair still does not will to be itself or in despair wills to be itself. Despair of the forgiveness of sins must be traceable to the one or to the other formula for despair, despair in weakness or the despair of defiance: despair in weakness, which is offended and does not dare to believe; the despair of defiance, which is offended and will not believe. But here weakness and defiance are the opposite of what they usually are (since here the point is not just about being oneself but about being oneself in the category of being a sinner, thus in the category of one's imperfection). Ordinarily weakness is: in despair not to will to be oneself. Here this is defiance, for here it is indeed the defiance of not willing to be oneself, what one is—a sinner—and for that reason wanting to dispense with the forgiveness of sins. Ordinarily defiance is: in despair to will to be oneself. Here this is weakness, in despair to will to be oneself—a sinner—in such a way that there is no forgiveness.

A self directly before Christ is a self intensified by the inordinate concession from God, intensified by the inordinate accent that falls upon it because God allowed himself to be born, become man, suffer, and die also for the sake of this self. As stated previously, the greater the conception of God, the more self; so it holds true here: the greater the conception of

---

* Note the distinction between despairing *over* one's sin and despairing *of* the forgiveness of sins.[59]

Christ, the more self. Qualitatively a self is what its criterion is. That Christ is the criterion is the expression, attested by God, for the staggering reality that a self has, for only in Christ is it true that God is man's goal and criterion, or the criterion and goal. —But the more self there is, the more intense is sin.

The intensification of sin can also be shown from another side. Sin was despair, the intensification was despair over sin. But now God offers reconciliation in the forgiveness of sin. Nevertheless, the sinner still despairs, and despair acquires a still deeper manifestation: it now relates to God in a way, and yet precisely because it is even further away it is even more intensively absorbed in sin. When the sinner despairs of the forgiveness of sins, it is almost as if he walked right up to God and said, "No, there is no forgiveness of sins, it is impossible," and it looks like close combat. Yet to be able to say this and for it to be heard, a person must become qualitatively distanced from God, and in order to fight *cominus* [in close combat] he must be *eminus* [at a distance]—so wondrously is the life of the spirit acoustically constructed, so wondrously are the ratios of distance established.[60] In order that the "No," which in a way wants to grapple with God, can be heard, a person must get as far away from God as possible. The most offensive forwardness toward God is at the greatest distance; in order to be forward toward God, a person must go far away; if he comes closer, he cannot be forward, and if he is forward, this *eo ipso* means that he is far away. What human powerlessness directly before God! If a person is forward toward a man of rank and importance, he may very well be punished by being thrust far away from him, but in order to be able to be forward toward God, one has to go far away from him.

In life, this sin (to despair of the forgiveness of sins) is conceived erroneously more often than not, especially since the time when the ethical was abolished, so that an authentic ethical word is seldom or never heard. Despairing of the forgiveness of sins is esthetically-metaphysically esteemed as a sign of a deep nature, which is about the same as accepting naughtiness in a child as a sign of a deep nature. On the whole, it is unbelievable what confusion has entered the sphere of religion since the time when "thou shalt" was abolished as the sole regulative aspect of man's relationship to God. This "thou shalt" must be present in any determination of the religious; in its place, the God-idea or the concept of God has been fancifully used as an ingredient in human importance, in becoming self-important directly before God. Just as one becomes self-important in politics by belonging to the opposition and eventually comes to prefer to have an administration just to have something to oppose, so also there is eventually a reluctance to do away with God—just to become even more self-important by being the opposition. Everything that in the old days was regarded with horror as the expression of ungodly insubordination is now regarded as genius, the sign of a deep nature. "Thou shalt believe" is the old-fashioned phrase, short and good, as sober as possible—nowadays it is a sign of genius and a deep nature not to be able to do so. "Thou shalt believe in the forgiveness of sins" were the words, and the only commentary on that was "You will harm yourself if you cannot do it, for one can do what one is supposed to do"[61]— nowadays it is a sign of genius and of a deep nature not to be able to believe that. What an excellent outcome Christendom has brought about! If not one word about Christianity were heard, men would not be so conceited, something paganism has never been; but since the Christian conceptions float unchristianly in the air, they have been used for the most aggravated rudeness—if not misused in some other but equally shameless manner. Is it not epigrammatic enough that cursing was not customary in paganism, whereas it really is right at home in Christendom, that out of a kind of horror and fear of the mysterious paganism as a rule named the name of God with tremendous solemnity, whereas in Christendom God's name is the word that most frequently appears in daily speech and is clearly the word that is given the least thought and used most carelessly, because the poor, revealed God (who instead of keeping himself hidden, as the upper class usually does, was careless and injudicious enough to become revealed) has become a personage far too familiar to the whole population, a personage for whom they then do the exceedingly great service of going to church every once in a while, for which they are also commended by the pastor, who on behalf of God thanks them for the honor of the visit, favors them with the title of pious, but is a little sarcastic about those who never show God the honor of going to church.

The sin of despairing of the forgiveness of sins is *offense.* The Jews had a perfect right to be offended by Christ because he claimed to forgive sins.[62] It takes a singularly high degree of spiritlessness (that is, as ordinarily found in Christendom), if one is not a believer (and if one is a believer, one does believe that Christ was God), not to be offended at someone's claim to forgive sins. And in the next place, it takes an equally singular spiritlessness not to be offended at the very idea that sin can be forgiven. For the human understanding, this is most impossible—but I do not therefore laud as genius the inability to believe it, for it *shall* be believed.

XI
226

In paganism, of course, this sin could not be found. If the pagan could have had the true conception of sin (which he could not even have, since he lacked the conception of God), he could not have gone any further than to despair over his sin. Indeed, more than that (and herein is all the concession that can be made to human understanding and thought), the pagan must be eulogized who actually reached the point of despairing not over the world, not over himself in general, but over his sin.* Humanly speaking, it takes both depth and ethical qualifications for that. Further than this, no human being as such can come, and rarely does anyone come so far.

---

* Note that here despair over sin is dialectially understood as pointing toward faith. The existence of this dialectic must never be forgotten (even though this book deals only with despair as sickness); in fact, it is implied in despair's also being the first element in faith. But when the direction is away from faith, away from the God-relationship, then despair over sin is the new sin. In the life of the spirit, everything is dialectical. Indeed, offense as annulled possibility is an element in faith, but offense directed away from faith is sin. That a person never once is capable of being offended by Christianity can be held against him. To speak that way implies that being offended is something good. But it must be said that to be offended is sin.

But, Christianly, everything is changed, for you shall believe in the forgiveness of sins.

And what is the situation of Christendom with regard to the forgiveness of sins? Well, the state of Christendom is actually despair of the forgiveness of sins; but this must be understood in the sense that Christendom is so far behind that its state never becomes apparent as being that. Even the consciousness of sin is not reached, and the only kinds of sins recognized are those that paganism also recognized—and life goes on happily in pagan peace of mind. By living in Christendom, however, men go beyond paganism, they go ahead and imagine that this peace of mind is—well, it cannot be otherwise in Christendom—consciousness of the forgiveness of sins, a notion that the clergy encourage the congregation to believe.

XI
227

Christendom's basic trouble is really Christianity, that the teaching about the God-man (please note that, Christianly understood, this is safeguarded by the paradox and the possibility of offense) is profaned by being preached day in and day out, that the qualitative difference between God and man is pantheistically abolished (first in a highbrow way through speculation, then in a lowbrow way in the highways and byways).[63] No teaching on earth has ever really brought God and man so close together as Christianity, nor can any do so, for only God himself can do that, and any human fabrication remains just a dream, a precarious delusion. But neither has any teaching ever protected itself so painstakingly against the most dreadful of all blasphemies, that after God has taken this step it should be taken in vain, as if it all merges into one—God and man—never has any teaching been protected in the same way as Christianity, which protects itself by means of the offense. Woe to the babblers, woe to the loose thinkers, and woe, woe to all the hangers-on who have learned from them and praised them!

If order is to be maintained in existence—and God does want that, for he is not a God of confusion[64]—then the first thing to keep in mind is that every human being is an individual human being and is to become conscious of being an indi-

vidual human being. If men are first permitted to run together
in what Aristotle calls the animal category[65]—the crowd—
then this abstraction, instead of being less than nothing, even
less than the most insignificant individual human being, comes
to be regarded as being something—then it does not take long
before this abstraction becomes God.[66] And then, *philosophice*
[philosophically viewed], the doctrine of the God-man is correct. Then, just as we have learned that in governments the
masses intimidate the king and the newspapers intimidate the
cabinet ministers, so we have finally discovered that the
summa summarum [sum total] of all men intimidates God. This

is then called the doctrine of the God-man, or that God and
man are *idem per idem* [the same]. Of course, some of the philosophers who were involved in spreading the teaching about
the predominance of the generation over the individual turn
away in disgust when their teaching has so degenerated that
the mob is the God-man. But these philosophers forget that it
is still their doctrine; they ignore that it was not more true
when the upper class accepted it, when the elite of the upper
class accepted it, when the elite of the upper class or a select
circle of philosophers was the incarnation.

This means that the doctrine of the God-man has made
Christendom brazen. It almost seems as if God were too
weak. It seems as if the same thing happened to him as happens to the good-natured person who makes too great concessions and then is repaid with ingratitude. It is God who de-
vised the teaching about the God-man, and now Christendom
has brazenly turned it around and foists kinship on God, so
that the concession that God has made means practically what
it means these days when a king grants a more independent
constitution—and we certainly know what that means: "he
was forced to do it."[67] It seems as if God had gotten himself
into hot water; it seems as if the sensible man would be right
if he said to God: It is your own fault. Why did you get so
involved with man? It would never have occurred to any
man, it would never have arisen in any man's heart[68] that
there should be this likeness between God and man. It was

you yourself who had it announced—now you are reaping the harvest.

But Christianity has protected itself from the beginning. It begins with the teaching about sin. The category of sin is the category of individuality. Sin cannot be thought speculatively at all. The individual human being lies beneath the concept; an individual human being cannot be thought, but only the concept "man." —That is why speculation promptly embarks upon the teaching about the *predominance* of the generation over the individual, for it is too much to expect that speculation should acknowledge the *impotence* of the concept in relation to actuality. —But just as one individual person cannot be thought, neither can one individual sinner; sin can be thought (then it becomes negation), but not one individual sinner. That is precisely why there is no earnestness about sin if it is only to be thought, for earnestness is simply this: that you and I are sinners. Earnestness is not sin in general; rather, the accent of earnestness rests on the sinner, who is the single individual. With respect to "the single individual," speculation, if it is consistent, must make light of being a single individual or being that which cannot be thought. If it cares to do anything along this line, it must say to the individual: Is this anything to waste your time on? Forget it! To be an individual human being is to be nothing! Think—then you are all mankind: *cogito ergo sum* [I think therefore I am].[69] But perhaps that is a lie; perhaps instead the single individual human being and to be a single human being are the highest. Just suppose it is. To be completely consistent, then, speculation must also say: To be an individual sinner is not to be something; it lies beneath the concept; do not waste any time on it etc. And what then? Instead of being an individual sinner, is one to think sin (just as one is asked to think the concept "man" instead of being an individual human being)? And what then? By thinking sin, does a person himself become "sin"—*cogito ergo sum*? A brilliant suggestion! But there is no need to fear that one will become sin—pure sin—in this way, for sin cannot be thought. Even speculation has to admit this, inasmuch

XI
229

as sin does indeed fall outside the concept "sin." But let us terminate this arguing *e concessis* [on the basis of the opponent's premises]—the main issue is something else. Speculation does not take into consideration that with respect to sin the ethical is involved, always pointing in the direction opposite to that of speculation and taking the very opposite steps, for the ethical does not abstract from actuality but immerses itself in actuality and operates mainly with the help of that speculatively disregarded and scorned category: individuality. Sin is a qualification of the single individual; it is irresponsibility and new sin to pretend as if it were nothing to be an individual sinner—when one himself is this individual sinner. Here Christianity steps in, makes the sign of the cross before speculation; it is just as impossible for speculation to get around this issue as for a sailing vessel to sail directly against a contrary wind. The earnestness of sin is its actuality in the single individual, be it you or I. Speculatively, we are supposed to look away from the single individual; therefore, speculatively, we can speak only superficially about sin. The dialectic of sin is diametrically contrary to that of speculation.

Christianity begins here—with the teaching about sin, and thereby with the single individual.* Surely it is Christianity

---

* The teaching about the sin of the race has often been misused, because it has not been realized that sin, however common it is to all, does not gather men together in a common idea, into an association, into a partnership ("no more than the multitude of the dead out in the cemetery form some kind of society");[70] instead, it splits men up into single individuals and holds each individual fast as a sinner, a splitting up that in another sense is both harmonized with and teleologically oriented to the perfection of existence. This has not been observed, and thus the fallen race has been regarded as reconciled by Christ once and for all. And so once again God has been saddled with an abstraction that claims, as abstraction, to have a closer kinship with him. But this is a mask that merely makes men brazen. If "the single individual" is to feel in kinship with God (and this is what Christianity teaches), then he also senses the full weight of it in fear and trembling, and he must discover—as if it were not an ancient discovery—the possibility of offense. But if the single individual is to come to this glory by means of an abstraction, then the matter becomes too easy and is essentially prostituted. Then the individual does not sense the enormous weight of God, which through humiliation weighs one down as far as it lifts one up; by participating in that abstraction,

that has taught us about the God-man, about the likeness between God and man, but it has a great abhorrence of flippant or brazen forwardness. By means of the teaching about sin and particular sins, God and Christ, quite unlike any kings, have protected themselves once and for all against the nation, the people, the crowd, the public, etc. and also against every demand for a more independent constitution. All those abstractions simply do not exist for God; for God in Christ there live only single individuals (sinners). Yet God can very well encompass the whole; he can take care of the sparrows[71] to boot. God is indeed a friend of order, and to that end he is present in person at every point, is everywhere present at every moment (in the textbook this is listed as one of the attributes of God, something people think about a little once in a while but certainly never try to think about continuously). His concept is not like man's, beneath which the single individual lies as that which cannot be merged in the concept; his concept embraces everything, and in another sense he has no concept. God does not avail himself of an abridgment; he comprehends (*comprehendit*) actuality itself, all its particulars; for him the single individual does not lie beneath the concept.

The teaching about sin—that you and I are sinners—a teaching that unconditionally splits up "the crowd," confirms the qualitative difference between God and man more radically than ever before, for again only God can do this; sin is indeed: *before God*. In no way is a man so different from God as in this, that he, and that means every man, is a sinner, and is that "before God," whereby the opposites are kept together in a double sense: they are held together (*continentur*), they are not allowed to go away from each other, but by being held

XI
231

---

the individual fancies that he has everything as a matter of course. Being a human being is not like being an animal, for which the specimen is always less than the species. Man is distinguished from other animal species not only by the superiorities that are generally mentioned but is also qualitatively distinguished by the fact that the individual, the single individual, is more than the species. This qualification is in turn dialectical and signifies that the single individual is a sinner, but then again that it is a perfection to be the single individual.

together in this way the differences show up all the more
sharply, just as when two colors are held together, *opposita
juxta se posita magis illucesunt* [the opposites appear more
clearly by juxtaposition]. Sin is the one and only predication
about a human being that in no way, either *via negationis* [by
denial] or *via eminentiæ* [by idealization],[72] can be stated of
God. To say of God (in the same sense as saying that he is not
finite and, consequently, *via negationis*, that he is infinite) that
he is not a sinner is blasphemy.

As sinner, man is separated from God by the most chasmic
qualitative abyss. In turn, of course, God is separated from
man by the same chasmic qualitative abyss when he forgives
sins. If by some kind of reverse adjustment the divine could
be shifted over to the human, there is one way in which man
could never in all eternity come to be like God: in forgiving
sins.

At this point lies the most extreme concentration of offense,
and this has been found necessary by the very doctrine that
has taught the likeness between God and man.

However, offense is the most decisive qualification of sub-
jectivity, of the single individual, that is possible. To think offense without thinking a person offended is perhaps not as
impossible as thinking flute playing when there is no flute
player,[73] but even thought has to admit that offense, even
more than falling in love, is an illusive concept that does not
become actual until someone, a single individual, is offended.

Thus offense is related to the single individual. And with
this, Christianity begins, that is, with making every man a
single individual, an individual sinner; and here everything
that heaven and earth can muster regarding the possibility of
offense (God alone has control of that) is concentrated—and
this is Christianity. Then Christianity says to each individual:
You shall believe—that is, either you shall be offended or you
shall believe. Not one word more; there is nothing more to
add. "Now I have spoken," declares God in heaven; "we shall
discuss it again in eternity. In the meantime, you can do what
you want to, but judgment is at hand."

A judgment! Of course, we men have learned, and experience teaches us, that when there is a mutiny on a ship or in an army there are so many who are guilty that punishment has to be abandoned, and when it is the public, the esteemed, cultured public, or a people, then there is not only no crime, then, according to the newpapers (upon which we can depend as upon the gospel and revelation), then it is God's will. How can this be? It follows from the fact that the concept "judgment" corresponds to the single individual; judgment is not made *en masse*. People can be put to death *en masse*, can be sprayed *en masse*, can be flattered *en masse*—in short, in many ways they can be treated as cattle, but they cannot be judged as cattle, for cattle cannot come under judgment. No matter how many are judged, if the judging is to have any earnestness and truth, then each individual is judged.* Now when so many are guilty, it is humanly impossible to do it—that is why the whole thing is abandoned. It is obvious that there can be no judgment: there are too many to be judged; it is impossible to get hold of them or manage to get hold of them as single individuals, and therefore *judging* has to be abandoned.

XI
233

And now in our enlightened age, when all anthropomorphic and anthropopathic conceptions of God are inappropriate, it is still not inappropriate to think of God as a judge comparable to an ordinary district judge or judge advocate who cannot get through such a complicated and protracted case—and the conclusion is that it will be exactly like this in eternity. Therefore, let us just stick together and make sure that the clergy preach this way. And should there happen to be an individual who dares to speak otherwise, an individual foolish enough to make his own life concerned and accountable in fear and trembling, and then in addition makes himself a nuisance to others—then let us protect ourselves by regarding him as mad or, if necessary, by putting him to death. If many of us do it, then there is no wrong. It is nonsense, an antiquated notion, that the many can do wrong. What many do is God's will. Before this wisdom—this we know from

* This is why God is "the judge," because for him there is no crowd, only single individuals.

experience, for we are not inexperienced striplings; we do not talk glibly, we speak as men of experience—before this wisdom to this day all men have bowed—kings, emperors, and excellencies—by means of this wisdom all our animals have been improved up to now—and so you can wager that God, too, is going to learn to bow. It is just a matter of continuing to be many, a good majority who stick together; if we do that, then we are protected against the judgment of eternity.

Well, presumably they would be protected if they were not supposed to become single individuals except in eternity. But before God they were and are continually single individuals; the person sitting in a showcase is not as embarrassed as every human being is in his transparency before God. This is the relationship of conscience. The arrangement is such that through the conscience the report promptly follows each guilt, and the guilty one himself must write it. But it is written with invisible ink and therefore first becomes clearly legible only when it is held up to the light in eternity while eternity is auditing the consciences. Essentially, everyone arrives in eternity bringing along with him and delivering his own absolutely accurate record of every least trifle he has committed or omitted. Thus a child could hold court in eternity; there is really nothing for a third party to do, everything down to the most insignificant word spoken is in order. The situation of the guilty person traveling through life to eternity is like that of the murderer who fled the scene of his act—and his crime—on the express train: alas, just beneath the coach in which he sat ran the telegraph wires carrying his description and orders for his arrest at the first station. When he arrived at the station and left the coach, he was arrested—in a way, he had personally brought his own denunciation along with him.

Therefore, despair of the forgiveness of sins is offense. And offense is the intensification of sin. Usually people give this scarcely a thought, usually never identify offense with sin, of which they do not speak; instead, they speak of sins, among which offense does not find a place. Even less do they perceive offense as the intensification of sin. That is because the opposites are construed not as being sin/faith but as sin/virtue.

C.

THE SIN OF DISMISSING CHRISTIANITY *MODO PONENDO*   XI
[POSITIVELY], OF DECLARING IT TO BE UNTRUTH   234

This is sin against the Holy Spirit. Here the self is at the highest intensity of despair; it not only discards Christianity totally but also makes it out to be a lie and untruth. What a tremendously despairing conception of itself the self must have!

The intensification of sin appears clearly if it is conceived as being a war between man and God in which the tactics are changed; the intensification is an ascent from the defensive to the offensive. Sin is despair; here the battle is by way of evasion. Then comes despair over one's sin; here again the battle is by way of evasion or a strengthening of one's retreating position, but always *pedem referens* [in retreat]. Now the tactic is changed; although sin digs down ever more deeply into itself, thus moving further away, yet in another sense it comes closer, becoming more and more decisively itself. Despair of the forgiveness of sins is a definite position over against an offer of God's mercy; sin is not solely retreat, not merely defensive action. But the sin of renouncing Christianity as untruth and a lie is offensive war. In a way, all the previous forms make the admission that the adversary is the stronger.   XI
But now sin is attacking.   235

Sin against the Holy Spirit[74] is the positive form of being offended.

Christian doctrine is the teaching about the God-man, about the kinship between God and man, but of such a nature, please note, that the possibility of offense is, if I may say it this way, the guarantee whereby God protects himself against man's coming too close. The possibility of offense is the dialectical element in everything essentially Christian. If this is taken away, then Christianity is not only paganism but also something so fanciful that paganism would have to call it nonsense. To be so close to God, as Christianity teaches that man can come to him, dares come to him, and shall come to him in Christ—such a thought never occurred to any man. Now if this is to be understood directly, taken at face value without the least little reservation and in an utterly jaunty and cavalier fashion, then Christianity—if we call paganism's fiction of the gods human madness—is an invention of a mad god. A man who still preserves his understanding must come to the verdict that only a god bereft of understanding could concoct such a teaching. The incarnate God, if without further ado one were to be hail-fellow-well-met with him, would then become a counterpart of Shakespeare's Prince Henry.[75]

God and man are two qualities separated by an infinite qualitative difference. Humanly speaking, any teaching that disregards this difference is demented—divinely understood, it is blasphemy. In paganism, man made god a man (the man-god); in Christianity God makes himself man (the God-man). But in this infinite love of his merciful grace he nevertheless makes one condition: he cannot do otherwise. Precisely this is Christ's grief, that "he cannot do otherwise";[76] he can debase himself, take a servant's form, suffer, die for men, invite all to come to him,[77] offer up every day of his life, every hour of the day, and offer up his life—but he cannot remove the possibility of offense. What a rare act of love, what unfathomable grief of love, that even God cannot remove the possibility that this act of love reverses itself for a person and becomes the most extreme misery—something that in another sense God does not want to do, cannot want to do. The

greatest possible human misery, greater even than sin, is to be offended at Christ and to continue in the offense; and Christ cannot, "love" cannot, make this impossible. This, you see, is why he says: "Blessed is he who is not offended at me."[78] More he cannot do. Therefore he can—it is possible—he can by his love make a person as miserable as one otherwise never could be. What an unfathomable conflict in love! Yet in love he does not have the heart to desist from completing this act of love—alas, even though it makes a person more miserable than he otherwise would ever have been!

Let us speak about this very humanly. How pitiable is the person who has never been motivated by love to sacrifice everything for the sake of love and consequently has never been able to do it! But suppose he discovered that precisely this, his love-motivated sacrifice, could become the greatest unhappiness for another person, for the beloved—what then? One of two things would happen. Either his love would lose its resiliency—from being a life force, it would subside into a brooding over mournful feelings closed up within; he would give up love, would not dare to perform this act of love, even collapsing, not under the act, but under the weight of that possibility. Just as a weight becomes ever so much heavier when it is placed on the end of a rod and the lifter has to hold it by the opposite end, so every act becomes ever so much heavier when it becomes dialectical, and heaviest of all when it becomes sympathetic-dialectical, so that what love motivates him to do, a concern for the beloved seems in another sense to dissuade from doing. —Or love would conquer, and he would venture the act out of love. But in the joyousness of love (as love is always joyous, particularly when it sacrifices everything), there would still be a profound grief—for it was indeed possible! Therefore, he would complete his work of love, he would make the sacrifice (in which he for his part would exult) but not without tears: there hovers over this— what should it be called, this historical painting of the inner life—that gloomy possibility. And yet, had this not hovered over it, his act would not have been an act of true love. —O, my friend, how have you been tried in life! Cudgel your brain, tear away every covering in your breast and expose the viscera of feeling, demolish every defense that separates you from the person you are reading about, and then read Shakespeare—and you will be appalled at the collisions. But even Shakespeare seems to have recoiled from essentially religious collisions. Indeed, perhaps these can be expressed only in the language of the gods. And no human being can speak this language. As a Greek has already said so beautifully: From men, man learns to speak, from the gods, to be silent.[79]

XI
237

The existence of an infinite qualitative difference between God and man constitutes the possibility of offense, which cannot be removed. Out of love, God becomes man. He says: Here you see what it is to be a human being; but he adds:

Take care, for I am also God—blessed is he who takes no offense at me. As man he takes a lowly servant's form; he shows what it is to be an unimportant man so that no man will feel himself excluded or think that it is human status and popularity with men that bring a person closer to God. No, he is the insignificant man. Look this way, he says, and know for certain what it is to be a human being, but take care, for I am also God—blessed is he who takes no offense at me. Or the reverse: The Father and I are one;[80] yet I am this simple, insignificant man, poor, forsaken, surrendered to man's violence[81]—blessed is he who takes no offense at me. I, this insignificant man, I am the one who makes the deaf hear, the blind see, the lame walk, the lepers clean, the dead rise up—blessed is he who takes no offense at me.[82]

Therefore, taking full responsibility, I venture to say that these words, "Blessed is he who takes no offense at me," belong in the proclamation about Christ, if not in the same way as the words of institution at the Lord's Supper, yet as the words "Let each man examine himself."[83] They are Christ's own words, and they must be declared again and again, especially in Christendom, must be repeated and addressed to each one individually. Wherever* these words are not pronounced also, or, in any case, wherever the presentation of Christianity is not penetrated at every point by this thought, Christianity is blasphemy. For without a bodyguard and servants to prepare the way for him and make men aware of who it was who was coming, Christ walked here on earth in the form of a lowly servant. But the possibility of offense (what a grief to him in his love!) defended and defends him, confirms a chas-

XI
238

XI
237

* And at present this is the case practically everywhere in Christendom, which seems *either* to ignore completely that Christ himself is the one who so repeatedly and fervently warned against offense, at the very end of his life warning even his loyal apostles,[84] who had followed him from the beginning and for his sake had forsaken everything—*or* tacitly to regard it as kind of exaggerated anxiety on Christ's part, since the experience of thousands upon thousands confirms that one can have faith in Christ without having noticed the slightest possibility of offense. But this may be an error that no doubt will come to light when the possibility of offense judges Christendom.

mic abyss between him and the person who was closest and stood closest to him.

The person who does not take offense *worships* in faith. But to worship, which is the expression of faith, is to express that the infinite, chasmic, qualitative abyss between them is confirmed. For in faith the possibility of offense is again the dialectical factor.*

But the kind of offense being discussed here is *modo ponendo* [positive]; it asserts that Christianity is untrue and a lie and thereby, in turn, says the same about Christ.

In order to characterize this kind of offense, it is best to look at the different forms of offense, which is related primarily to the paradox (Christ) and thus arises with every determination of the essentially Christian, for every such determination is related to Christ, has Christ *in mente* [in mind].

The lowest form of offense, the most innocent form, humanly speaking, is to leave the whole issue of Christ undecided, concluding as follows: I am not going to make any decision about it; I do not believe, but I am not going to decide anything. That this is a form of offense escapes most people, who have completely forgotten this Christian *"You shall."* Therefore they do not see that this, to be neutral about Christ, is offense. That Christianity is proclaimed to you means that you shall have an opinion about Christ; He is, or the fact that He exists and that He has existed is the decision about all existence. If Christ is proclaimed to you, then it is offense to say: I do not want to have any opinion about it.

XI
239

---

* Here is a little task for the observers. If it is assumed that all the many clergymen here and abroad who deliver and write sermons are believing Christians, how can it be explained that one never hears or reads the prayer that in our day especially is so appropriate: "God in heaven, I thank you for not requiring a person to comprehend Christianity, for if that were required, I would be the most miserable of all.[85] The more I seek to comprehend it, the more incomprehensible it appears to me and the more I discover only the possibility of offense. Therefore I thank you for requiring only faith, and I pray that you will continue to increase it."[86] As for orthodoxy, this prayer would be entirely correct and, given the sincerity of the one who prayed it, would also be the proper irony upon all speculation. But I wonder whether faith is to be found on earth![87]

XI
238

This must be understood with certain restrictions in these times when the preaching of Christianity is as mediocre as it is. No doubt there are many thousands today who have heard Christianity proclaimed and have never heard a thing about this "shall." But if the person who has heard it says: I do not want to have any opinion about it, then he is offended. He is denying the very divinity of Christ, that He has the right to lay upon a person the claim that he shall have an opinion. It does not help for him to say, "I am not saying anything, neither 'yes' nor 'no,' about Christ," for then the next question is: Do you have no opinion as to whether you *shall* have an opinion about him or not? If he answers "yes" to that, he traps himself; and if he answers "no," then Christianity makes the decision for him anyway, that he *shall* have an opinion about it and thus in turn about Christ, that no man shall presume to leave Christ's life in abeyance as a curiosity. When God lets himself be born and become man, this is not an idle caprice, some fancy he hits upon just to be doing something, perhaps to put an end to the boredom that has brashly been said must be involved in being God[88]—it is not in order to have an adventure. No, when God does this, then this fact is the earnestness of existence. And, in turn, the earnestness in this earnestness is: that everyone *shall* have an opinion about it. When a king visits a town in the provinces, he regards it as an insult if a public official fails, without sufficient cause, to pay his respects to him; but I wonder what he would think if someone were to ignore completely the fact that the king was in town and played the private citizen who says: "The devil take His Majesty and the Royal Law."[89] And so also when it pleases God to become man—and then it pleases someone (and what the public official is before the king every person is before God) to say: Well, this is something I do not care to form any opinion about. This is the way a man talks pretentiously about what he basically ignores—and thus pretentiously ignores God.

The next form of offense is negative but in the form of being acted upon, of suffering. It definitely feels that it cannot ignore Christ, is not capable of leaving Christ in abeyance and

XI
240

then otherwise leading a busy life. But neither can it believe; it continues to stare fixedly and exclusively at one point, at the paradox. It honors Christianity insofar as it expresses that the question "What do you think of Christ?"[90] is actually the most crucial of all questions. A person so offended lives on as a shadow; his life is devastated because deep within himself he is constantly preoccupied with this decision. In this way he expresses what reality [*Realitet*] Christianity has (just as the suffering of unhappy love with respect to love).

The last form of offense is the one under discussion in this section, the positive form. It declares Christianity to be untrue, a lie; it denies Christ (that he has existed and that he is the one he said he was) either docetically or rationalistically, so that either Christ does not become an individual human being but only appears to be, or he becomes only an individual human being—thus, either he docetically becomes fiction, mythology, which makes no claim upon actuality, or he rationalistically becomes an actuality who makes no claim to be divine. Of course, in this denial of Christ as the paradox lies, in turn, the denial of all that is essentially Christian: sin, the forgiveness of sins, etc.

This form of offense is sin against the Holy Spirit. Just as the Jews said that Christ drove out devils with the help of devils,[91] so this offense makes Christ out to be an invention of the devil.

XI
241

This offense is the highest intensification of sin, something that is usually overlooked because the opposites are not construed Christianly as being sin/faith.

This contrast [sin/faith], however, has been advanced throughout this entire book, which at the outset introduced in Part One, A, A, the formula for the state in which there is no despair at all: in relating itself to itself and in willing to be itself, the self rests transparently in the power that established it. This formula in turn, as has been frequently pointed out, is the definition of faith.[92]

SUPPLEMENT

KEY TO REFERENCES

Marginal references alongside the text are to volume and page [XI 100] in *Søren Kierkegaard's samlede Værker*, I-XIV, edited by A. B. Drachmann, J. L. Heiberg, and H. O. Lange (1 ed., Copenhagen: Gyldendal, 1901-06). The same marginal references are used in Søren Kierkegaard, *Gesammelte Werke*, Abt. 1-36 (Düsseldorf: Diederichs Verlag, 1952-69).

References to Kierkegaard's works in English are to this edition, *Kierkegaard's Writings* [*KW*], I-XXVI (Princeton: Princeton University Press, 1978-). Specific references to the *Writings* are given by English title and the standard Danish pagination referred to above [*Either/Or*, I, *KW* III (*SV* I 100)].

References to the *Papirer* [*Pap*. I A 100; note the differentiating letter A, B, or C, used only in references to the *Papirer*] are to *Søren Kierkegaards Papirer*, I-XI³, edited by P. A. Heiberg, V. Kuhr, and E. Torsting (1 ed., Copenhagen: Gyldendal, 1909-48), and 2 ed., photo-offset with two supplemental volumes, I-XIII, edited by Niels Thulstrup (Copenhagen: Gyldendal, 1968-70), and with index, XIV-XVI (1975-78), edited by N. J. Cappelørn. References to the *Papirer* in English [*JP* II 1500] are to volume and serial entry number in *Søren Kierkegaard's Journals and Papers*, I-VII, edited and translated by Howard V. Hong and Edna H. Hong (Bloomington: Indiana University Press, 1967-78).

References to correspondence are to the serial numbers in *Breve og Aktstykker vedrørende Søren Kierkegaard*, I-II, edited by Niels Thulstrup (Copenhagen: Munksgaard, 1953-54), and to the corresponding serial numbers in *Kierkegaard: Letters and Documents*, translated by Henrik Rosenmeier, *Kierkegaard's Writings*, XXV [*Letters, KW* XXV, Letter 100].

References to books in Kierkegaard's own library [*ASKB* 100] are based on the serial numbering system of *Auktionsprotokol over Søren Kierkegaards Bogsamling* [Auction-catalog of Søren Kierkegaard's Book-collection], edited by H. P. Rohde (Copenhagen: Royal Library, 1967).

In the Supplement, references to page and lines in the text are given as: 100:1-10.

In the notes, internal references to the present work are given as: p. 100.

Three periods indicate an omission by the editors; five periods indicate a hiatus or fragmentariness in the text.

Sygdommen til Døden.

En christelig psychologisk Udvikling

til Opbyggelse og Opvækkelse.

Af

Anti-Climacus.

Udgivet af

S. Kierkegaard.

———⟨⬦⟩———

Kjøbenhavn 1849.

Paa Universitetsboghandler C. A. Reitzels Forlag.

Trykt hos Kgl. Hofbogtrykker Bianco Luno.

THE SICKNESS UNTO DEATH.

A Christian Psychological Exposition

for Upbuilding and Awakening.

By

Anti-Climacus.

Edited by

S. Kierkegaard.

Copenhagen 1849.

Published by University Bookseller C. A. Reitzel's Press.

Printed by the Royal Printer Bianco Luno.

SELECTED ENTRIES FROM
KIERKEGAARD'S JOURNALS AND PAPERS
PERTAINING TO
THE SICKNESS UNTO DEATH

Provisional title page; see pp. 136-37:

The Sickness unto Death
A Christian Psychological [*changed from*: Upbuilding]
Exposition [*deleted*: in the Form of a Discourse]
by
S. Kierkegaard
—*Pap.* VIII² B 140 *n.d.*, 1848

From final copy; see title page:

The book is to be printed in
small format like that of
"Philosophical Fragments"
but in brevier type.

The Sickness unto Death
A Christian Upbuilding [*changed to*: Psychological]
Exposition
[*Added*: For Upbuilding and Awakening]
by
S. Kierkegaard [*changed to*: Anticlimacus; *again*
changed to: Anti-Climacus]
[*Added*: edited by
S. Kierkegaard]

Copenhagen 1849
Published by University Bookseller Reitzel's Press
Printed by the Royal Printer Bianco Luno

—*Pap.* VIII² B 171:1-5 *n.d.*, 1848

From final copy; see 3:

N.B. Perhaps this can be placed on the overleaf.
[*Deleted*: A sermon by Bishop Albertini: See *Handbuch deutscher Beredsamkeit, v.* Dr. O.L.B. Wolff, Leipzig 1845, Pt. I, p. 293.]—*Pap.* VIII² B 171:6 *n.d.*, 1848

From final copy; see 5:

Preface

[*Added*: To the compositor
The smallest possible brevier.]
—*Pap.* VIII² B 171:7 *n.d.*, 1848

See 6:8:

[*In margin*: A passage in the preface to the book
The Sickness unto Death.]
To the closing passage, "But that the form is what it is," I have thought of adding:
apart from the fact that it is also rooted in my being who I am.

But this would be going too far in transforming a fictitious character into actuality; a fictitious character has no other possibility than the one he is; he cannot declare that he could also speak in another way and yet be the same; he has no identity that encompasses many possibilities.

On the other hand, the fact that he says: "It is at least well considered"—is proper, for it may very well be that, although it is his only form. For him to say: "It is psychologically correct" is a double blow, for it is also psychologically correct with respect to Anti-Climacus.

Climacus is lower, denies he is a Christian.[1] Anti-Climacus is higher, a Christian on an extraordinarily high level. [*In margin*: see p. 249 (*i.e., Pap.* X¹ A 517)]. With Climacus everything drowns in humor;[2] therefore he himself revokes his book.[3] Anti-Climacus is thetical.—*JP* VI 6439 (*Pap.* X¹ A 530) *n.d.*, 1849

From draft of Preface; see 6:20:

From "The Sickness unto Death":
Prayer

[*In margin:* N.B. Not to be used, perhaps, since a prayer here gives an almost too upbuilding tone.]

Father in heaven! So often the congregation brings its intercession to you for all who are sick and sorrowing; and if any of us is lying at death's door in mortal sickness, the congregation sometimes makes a special intercessory prayer: grant that each one of us may rightly become aware of which sickness is the sickness unto death, and of how we are all sick in this way! And you, our Lord Jesus Christ, you who came to the world to heal those who suffer from this sickness, which we all have but which you can heal only in those who are aware of being sick in this way: help us in this sickness to turn to you to be healed! And you, G·d the Holy Spirit, you who come to our assistance if we honestly want to be healed: be with us so that we never to our own ruination elude the physician's help but remain with him—saved from the sickness. For to be with him is to be saved from the sickness, and only when we are with him are we saved from the sickness!—*JP* III 3423 (*Pap.* VIII² B 143) *n.d.*, 1848

From final draft; see 13:1-14:2:

A. [*Part One*]
The Sickness unto Death Is Despair

[*In margin:* That Despair* Is the Sickness unto Death
Some Definitional Observations on Despair
and on the Expression the Sickness unto Death

*Note. No doubt this is unnecessary, but I will do it nevertheless: (*same as 6:14-16*). Despair is indeed that dialectical; it is the sickness unto death, and yet, from another side, it is the first form of the healing of that sickness (*same as 6:17-19*).

This note was used in the Preface.]⁴

A.

Despair is a sickness of the spirit, of the self, and consequently can take [changed from: *takes*] *three forms: in despair not to be conscious of having* [changed from: *conscious as*] *a self (not despair in the strict sense); in despair not to will to be oneself* [changed from: *in despair to want to get rid of one's self*]; *in despair to will to be oneself.*

1. [*Omitted from 13:11-15:* and in relating itself to itself relates itself as derived to a third.] A human being is a psychosomatic synthesis, a synthesis of the infinite and the finite . . ..

2. The human self [*same as 13:31-14:2*] another, and this is why there can be two [*changed from:* three] forms of despair in the strict sense.—*Pap.* VIII² B 170:1 *n.d.*, 1848

From final draft; see 14:29-32:

. . . The formula that expresses the condition in which there is no despair is this: when the self, in relating itself to itself and in willing to be itself, transparently rests in the power that established it (God).

3. [*See 14:24-25*] Despair is a misrelation in a relation that relates itself to itself; it is not a misrelation in a relation but in a relation that relates itself to itself. That is, despair is a qualification of spirit.

3. Despair is a sickness of the self. This is apparent in the fact that basically all despair is encompassed in one formula: to despair over oneself. A person in despair despairs over something.

cf. in the original manuscript, A. c.[5]

—*Pap.* VIII² B 170:2 *n.d.*, 1848

From final draft; see 14:34:

The Possibility and Actuality [deleted: *The Dialectic*] *of Despair* [deleted: *It Is Responsibility, Based on Its Being a Qualification of "Spirit," since It Is Not the Misrelation in the Relation between Two but in the Relation between Two That Is a Relation to Itself*].—*Pap.* VIII² B 170:3 *n.d.*, 1848

From draft; see 15:5:

. . . . . and something even more magnificent, that incomprehensible compounding, that eternal structuring of man, that he is compounded of the temporal and the eternal, that he, as man in kinship with the animal, is again as man in kinship with the divine.—*Pap.* VIII² B 168:2 *n.d.*, 1848

From draft; see 15:35-36:

. . . . . misrelation in the relation of a synthesis that relates itself to itself, between the temporal and the eternal in the human being compounded of the temporal and the eternal.—*Pap.* VIII² B 168:3 *n.d.*, 1848

From final draft; see 15:38:

. . . . . in the synthesis lies the possibility of the misrelation, and the responsibility lies in this, that the misrelation is in a relation that relates itself to itself in the qualification of spirit.—*Pap.* VIII² B 170:4 *n.d.*, 1848

From draft; see 16:6-22:

. . . . . if he were not a synthesis composed of the temporal and the eternal, he could not despair at all; and if he were not properly composed originally of the temporal and the eternal, he could not despair, either. Thus despair in man is a misrelation between the temporal and the eternal, of which his nature is composed—but from God's hand in the right relation.

From what, then, does the misrelation come? From the man himself, who disturbs the relation, which is precisely to despair. How is this possible? Quite simple. In the composite of the eternal and the temporal, man is a relation, in this relation itself and relating itself to itself. God made man a relation; to be a human being is to be a relation. But a relation which, by the very fact that God, as it were, releases it from his hand,[6] or the same moment God, as it were, releases it, is itself, relates itself to itself—this relation can become in the same moment a misrelation. To despair is the misrelation taking place.—*JP* I 68 (*Pap.* VIII² B 168:5) *n.d.*, 1848

From final draft; see 16:9-22:

Where, then, does the despair come from? From the relation in which the synthesis relates itself to itself. This relation is spirit, the self, and upon it rests the responsibility for all despair at every moment of its existence—however much the despairing person speaks of his despair as of a misfortune—just as in that previously mentioned case of dizziness, with which despair on the whole has much in common, so that one can say that dizziness, in the category of the psychical, corresponds to what despair is in the category of spirit. But the category of responsibility corresponds to the category of spirit. God constituted man as a relation, but when this relation relates itself to itself, God releases it from his hand,[7] as it were. In this way the human being is a self, and the misrelation is possible.—*Pap.* VIII² B 170:5 *n.d.*, 1848

From draft; see 16:19-22 ff.:

VIII⁷
B 168:6
260

. . . (b) *Despair Is Like Being Dizzy or Dizziness, Yet Essentially (Qualitatively) Different*

1. The possibility of dizziness lies in the composite of the psychical and the physical, an ambiguous joint boundary between the psychical and the physical. . . . Thus dizziness is an interplay of the psychical and the physical, even where it is easier to decide which is primarily active, although in many cases it is very difficult to decide.

VIII²
B 168:6
261

2. What dizziness is with respect to the composite of the psychical and the physical, despair is in things of the spirit, with respect to that composite of the finite and the infinite, freedom and necessity, the divine and the human in a relation which is [reflectively and responsibly] for itself [*for sig*].[8] The relation between the psychical and the physical, although a relation, is not (like despair) a relation which is for itself. This is

how it happens, as was shown, that the despairing person who, like the dizzy person in the moment of dizziness, is not himself master in the moment of despair, yet is responsible for his position in despair, something the one who is dizzy cannot in the same way be said to be.

With respect to despair, just as with respect to dizziness, it is sometimes easier to show which of the composites is primarily active, sometimes very difficult. But in all despair there is an interplay of finitude and infinitude, of the divine and the human, of freedom and necessity. Thus, to take an example of what will be developed later, a man despairs over [*over*] necessity, that is, when despair makes its appearance, necessity has become apparent to him in all its iciness. But nevertheless he despairs by virtue of freedom; it is, indeed, freedom which despairs. But now suppose that he despairs of [*om*] his freedom. Well, the interplay is there just the same; for in despairing of his freedom, necessity in one form or another must have become apparent to him. And yet it is by virtue of freedom that he despairs—of freedom. Consequently in all despair there is an interplay, since it [despair] is a misrelation in [a synthesis of components] which have a relation to one another or which are in a relation to one another or in that which constitutes the relation to one another, only that this misrelation is always responsible. A person can be afflicted with dizziness but never with despair.

3. In observing a person who is afflicted with dizziness, one will note, as is known, something remarkable in his appearance (symptomatic). A person thus afflicted often complains that something has fallen upon him, that it is as if he had a weight to bear, etc. This pressure, this weight, is not anything external; it is, as one says of an optical and an acoustical illusion, a nervous delusion, it is an inverse reflection of something internal; the sufferer feels an inward pressure as something external. It is the same with despair. The despairing person understands his despair as a suffering—instead of its being a guilt. This belongs so essentially to all despair, simply as a more extreme (but of course responsible) result of becoming and being in the state of despair, that it is a sign of

VIII²
B 168:6
262

healing and the beginning of deliverance if the despairing person learns to understand this differently. But as a neurotic complains about that external pressure, so the despairing person complains about despair and does not hear that it is—a self-accusation.

4. If one were to follow up the countless expressions of dizziness, he would always find that which corresponds to despair, he would always find in dizziness a similarity to despair. And many times this similarity can excellently illustrate and illuminate—indeed, in describing his situation, the person who despairs often resorts to expressions which are related to dizziness. It is only a similarity. The difference is infinite; the difference is that despair is related to spirit, to freedom, to responsibility.

5. In a healthy state or when there is equilibrium between the psychical and the physical, a man is never dizzy. It is the same with despair. If a man in relating himself to himself relates himself absolutely to God, there is no despair at all; but at every moment when this is not the case, there is also some despair. Consequently when a man in relating himself to himself absolutely relates himself to God, then all despair is annihilated. To an extent this differs from dizziness, because dizziness is a qualification of the human being psychically defined and is only a question of an equilibrium in the relation between the psychical and the physical, or, where this is disturbed, a question of bringing it about, whether the physical is primarily affected or the psychical, but where it is not a question of this relation's being for itself and thus also not a question of this relation's relating itself to a third. In the relation between two, the relation is in a certain sense a third; but if this relation is not for itself, then the relation is the third, but the relation is not a relation to a third. On the other hand, with respect to despair it is not a matter merely of equilibrium between the two, or, more accurately, the human being as spirit simply cannot have equilibrium in himself. He is, as the composite (the synthesis), a relation, but a relation which relates itself to itself. Yet he has not established himself as a relation; the relation which he is, even though a relation for itself,

VIII²
B 168:6
263

is established by another. Only by the relation to this other can he be in equilibrium. As soon as there is a misrelation in the relation, there is despair, but as soon as he does not in the relation relate himself to the other, there is also despair.

This last formula for despair does not merely indicate a special kind; on the contrary, all despair can ultimately be resolved in this, can be traced back to this. If the person who despairs is, as he believes, aware of his despair, he no longer speaks senselessly about it as something which happens to him, and now with all his might he will fight against it, but if he is not aware that the sickness lies still deeper, that the misrelation in him also reflects itself infinitely in the misrelation to the power which established him as a relation—then he is still in the despair, and with all his supposed labor he only works himself into an even deeper despair; he loses himself in despair and is again guilty and responsible for it.

Thus despair is essentially (qualitatively) different from dizziness. Yet perhaps this comparison, which neither depends upon a vagabond whim nor presents merely a fugitive resemblance but is as well considered as it is pregnant with analogies, probably has its deeper meaning.—*JP* I 749 (*Pap.* VIII² B 168:6) *n.d.*, 1848

VIII²
B 168:6
264

From final draft; see 17:20:

6. By despairing (for this is the retracing of actuality to possibility), the person is freely in the power of an alien force, is freely or in freedom slaving under it, or he is freely-unfreely in his own power. If one calls the alien force the master, then the person in despair is free in self-inflicted slaving for this master. And if one says that he is unfree in his own hands, he consequently slaves for himself, is his own slave. This is the misrelation. The true relation of freedom is this: freely to be completely in the power of the good, of freedom, or in the power of that in whose power one can be only by being free and through being in whose power one becomes free.[9] The second relation is this: freely serving, serving completely, to be simply an instrument in the power of the master, who no

doubt demands greater obedience than any master ever demanded of his slave but who nevertheless will not have any slave in his service.—*Pap.* VIII² B 170:6 *n.d.*, 1848

From final draft; see 17:21:

[*Deleted:* C.

Despair Elucidated by Comparison with the Nevertheless Qualitatively Different: Dizziness or Vertigo

1. The possibility of dizziness lies in the synthesis of the psychical and the physical as a relation (but not as a relation that relates itself to itself, which is a qualification of spirit). Dizziness is an ambiguous boundary between the psychical and the physical. Physicians know this very well, also that it is sometimes very difficult to decide which of the interacting elements is dominant. There is a dizziness that is caused by the physical and that from this point of departure influences the psychical, so that certain abdominal conditions can continually predispose to dizziness. There is also another kind of dizziness, which may be called psychical dizziness, according to the common practice of giving names on the basis of the dominant part. Fainting or what is called swooning, to pass out, takes place because there is an effect upon the physical such that the physical participates by fainting.]

C.

Despair Is "The Sickness unto Death"

—*Pap.* VIII² 170:7 *n.d.*, 1848

In margin of draft; see 18:23:

. . . . . a poem by Ewald on suicide.[10]—*Pap.* VIII² B 145:3 *n.d.*, 1848

From draft; see 20:15-36:

To despair over oneself, in despair not to will to be oneself, in despair to will to be rid of oneself, in despair to will to devour oneself is the formula for all despair, to which also the other form of despair, in despair to will to be oneself, can be traced back, just as above, in the despair not to will to be oneself, to will to be rid of oneself, is traced back to: in despair to will to be oneself.—*JP* I 750 (*Pap*. VIII² B 168:8) *n.d.*, 1848

From draft, in brackets; see 25:19:

Even if one were to imagine a person who psychosomatically is in the most perfect health, this must still be regarded as despair.—*Pap*. VIII² B 148:4 *n.d.*, 1848

From draft; see 26:14-17:

Therefore*. . ..

In margin: *It must be noted, however, that even those who say they are in despair are not always actually in despair, since one can affect despair and one can also confuse despair, which is a qualification of spirit, with all kinds of transitory depression, distraction, etc., which pass away without reaching the point of despair.

It is as far as possible from being the case, and it must be noted furthermore that not even those who say they are in despair are actually in despair. It may be just mental depression, distraction, and the sufferer may still not be conscious as spirit. And if not, it is rather the case that the common view, which holds that one who says . . ..—*Pap*. VIII²B 148:6 *n.d.*, 1848

In margin of draft; see 32:7-11:

The will merely becomes more and more abstract, and if it does not at the same time also become just as concrete, it becomes more and more impotent, finally ceases to be will, becomes volatilized in promises and resolutions that amount to nothing—and thereby the same is the case with the self, whose will it is.—*Pap*. VIII² B 150:6 *n.d.*, 1848

In margin of draft; see 35:7:

If fantasized lives may be said to mortgage themselves to the devil, then despairing philistines mortgage themselves to the world.

They are sighted in an outward direction but blind inwardly. In relation to a spiritual person, they are like statues in relation to living human beings; to all appearances they are human beings, just as are elf maidens, who are hollow at the back.—*Pap.* VIII² B 150:7 *n.d.*, 1848

From draft; see 37:29:

Both forms are forms of an unhappy consciousness.[11]—*Pap.* VIII² B 150:8 *n.d.*, 1848

From draft; see 38:26-34:

. . . . . despairing. But for God all things are possible. . . .

A character in Shakespeare says it so well; he curses those who deprived him of the convenient way to despair. (John II or Richard II—must check) III, 3: . . .—*Pap.* VIII² B 150:9 *n.d.*, 1848

In margin of final copy; see 40:31:

what is the counterpart of nitrogen called?—*Pap.* VIII² B 171:10 *n.d.*, 1848

In margin of final copy; see 42:11:

regarded as an existential qualification and—*Pap.* VIII² B 171:12 *n.d.*, 1848

From draft; see 42:25:

Moreover, here the significance of the Socratic definition[12] that all sin is ignorance becomes manifest.—*Pap.* VIII² B 150:11 *n.d.*, 1848

Deleted from final copy; see 47:36:

(D)

—*Pap.* VIII² B 171:13 *n.d.*, 1848

From draft; see 49:5-9:

C.

The Forms of Despair

In this section I shall give a psychological description of the forms of despair as these appear in actuality, in actual persons, whereas in A [*29:26-42:8*] despair was treated abstractly, as if it were not the despair of any person, and in B [*42:9-49:15*] was developed in terms of consciousness as decisive in the definition of despair.—*Pap.* VIII² B 151 *n.d.*, 1848

From draft; see 49:9-17:

This conscious despair will now be worked out in greater detail, so that the object of reflection is the doubleness of consciousness that consciousness is consciousness of what despair is and consciousness of one's own condition, that it is despair. The opposite of despair is faith; therefore a constant reference to its dialectic is reflected in the schema.

(α) *Despair over the Earthly or over Something Earthly.*

—*Pap.* VIII² B 152 *n.d.*, 1848

In margin of draft; see 49:9-15:

Moreover, the opposite of being in despair is: faith. Therefore, the formula given above (A, A, 3 [*i.e., 14:29-32*]), which describes the condition in which all despair is eradicated, is altogether correct. This is the formula for faith: in relating itself to itself and in willing to be itself, the self rests transparently in the power that established it.—*Pap.* VIII² B 153:1 *n.d.*, 1848

In margin of draft; see 50:fn.21-22:

i.e., without giving her self, whatever it is that she may give her self to (for the man does indeed give himself but still looks after his self).—*Pap.* VIII² B 153:3 *n.d.*, 1848

In margin of draft; see 51:33-52:10:

He calls this: to despair. The fact that to despair means something else entirely, that it means to lose the eternal, not to lose the earthly or something earthly, that consequently, viewed in the light of truth, he lost infinitely much more, inflicted upon himself a loss in comparison with which the loss he talks about, the loss he suffers, is child's play—this is completely hidden from him.

In margin: that consequently, while he stands lamenting the loss of the earthly and despairs (but to lose the earthly is by no means to despair), he loses something else completely different, the eternal, which is to despair, that consequently he loses something completely different and infinitely more than what he is talking about, that strangely enough, without despairing, he inflicts upon himself a loss in comparison with which the loss he talks about is child's play . . . . .—*JP* I 747 (*Pap.* VIII² B 154:3) *n.d.*, 1848

From draft; see 60:29-61:10:

(2) *Despair* [deleted: *over*] *of the eternal or over oneself.*
Despair over the earthly or over something earthly was also despair of the eternal and over oneself insofar as it was despair, for this is indeed what all despair is. And it is linguistically correct to say: to despair *over* the earthly (the occasion),* *of* the eternal, but *over* oneself, because this again is another expression for the occasion of the despair, which in the concept is always *of* the eternal, while that *over* which there is despair can be almost anything. But a person who despairs** in this way is not aware of what, so to speak, is going on behind him; he thinks he is despairing over something earthly† and

yet he is despairing of the eternal, for the fact that he attributes such great worth to the earthly or to something earthly means precisely to despair of the eternal, or to carry this further: the fact that he places such great worth upon something earthly or that he first equates something earthly with everything earthly and thereby places such great worth upon the earthly means precisely to despair of the eternal.

*See A, c.[13]

**As he has been presented above,

†and talks constantly of that over which he despairs—*Pap.* VIII² B 155 *n.d.*, 1848

From draft; see 60: fn. 1-61:fn. 9:

For C, в, b, α, 2.[14]

We despair *over* that which binds us in despair—over a misfortune, over the earthly, over a capital loss, etc.—but we despair *of* that which, rightly understood, releases a person from despair of the eternal, of his salvation, etc. In relation to the self, one says both *of* and *over* oneself, because the self is so dialectical.

And the haziness, particularly in all the lower forms of despair and in almost every person in despair, is that he so passionately and clearly sees and knows *over* what he despairs, but *of* what he despairs evades him. The condition for healing is always this repenting *of*, and to what extent it would be possible to be in despair with an altogether clear consciousness of the "of what" could be a subtle question.*

*purely philosophically—*Pap.* VIII² B 156 *n.d.*, 1848

From draft; see 65:21:

But there is something curious about you. The true way to go is for you like a wall you run against. There is something curious about you. Spiritually you are like a flute player who, if he would play the note as it is, could play it but who always wants to make it elaborate, and therefore it becomes false.—*Pap.* VIII² B 157:3 *n.d.*, 1848

In margin of draft; see 66:34:

..... as when Richard III [*changed from*: II] orders the beating of drums in order not to hear his mother's reproaches, or he will seek forgetfulness .....
See the enclosed [i.e., *Pap.* VIII² B 158].—*Pap.* VIII² B 157:5 *n.d.*, 1848

From draft; see 66:13-67:4:

VIII²
B 158
253

For Part One, C, B, a, 2.[15]

In conclusion, let us take still another little look at the person of inclosing reserve, who in his inclosing reserve marks time on the spot. In inclosing reserve and in despair he does not will to be himself. It was something earthly, something in the composition of the self or the earthly—in short, something finite over which he despaired; he concentrated all his passion on that point, and he despaired. Perhaps it still could have been lifted cautiously, perhaps, perhaps; in any case it should have been taken over in faith. But he despaired. Yet only in the next moment does his despair become manifest, for he despairs over the fact that he was weak enough to despair. This he is unwilling to forget; he is unwilling to forget himself. Yes, it seems to him that it cannot be done, even if he would, since his self has now incurred a fundamental defect. [*Essentially the same as 66:15-67:4.*]

Here there is another form of inclosing reserve that I would still like to discuss, a kind of poet-existence in relation to the religious. This inclosing reserve, as an occasion to despair over something earthly or the earthly—and thereupon to despair over his weakness, of the eternal, over himself—is also: in despair not to will to be oneself. Such a self actually has a profound religious longing; the conception of God is taken up in the inclosing reserve and is the spring in the mountain fastness of inclosing reserve. But closed up within himself and in despair he continues to be; he cannot let go of the fixed point. He loves God above all, God who is his only consolation in

his secret agony—and yet he loves the agony and will not let
it go. In despair, he nevertheless does not will to be himself, is
unwilling in faith to penetrate the agony. But, like one who
became unhappy in erotic love and has thereby become a poet
and loftily and blessedly celebrates the happiness of love, he
becomes the poet of religiousness. He became unhappy in religiousness. He feels obscurely that what is required of him is
that he should let go of this agony—but this he cannot do,
that is, in the ultimate sense he still is unwilling, and here his
self ends in vagueness. Yet this poet's description of the
religious—just like that other poet's description of erotic
love—has a charm, a lyrical verve, an eloquence that no married man's and no His Reverence's presentations have. Nor is
what he says untrue, by no means; his presentation is simply
his happier, his better *I*. His relation to the religious is that of
an unhappy lover, not, in the strictest sense, that of a believer;
he has only the first element of faith—despair—and within it
an intense longing for the religious.—*Pap.* VIII² B 158 *n.d.*,
1848

VIII²
B 158
254

From draft; see 71:31:

Thus it appears that much of what is embellished in the
world under the name of resignation is often this kind of *despair* (such as suffering or a situation occasioning suffering): in
despair to will to be oneself, in despair to want to comfort
oneself by becoming more and more abstract, in despair to
will to make the eternal suffice and thereby to be able to defy
the earthly and the temporal. . . .—*JP* I 748 (*Pap.* VIII² B
159:4) *n.d.*, 1848

From draft; see 77:11-78:31:

For Part Two, A
To be used as an example of a remarkable frontier between
the first and second parts, therefore in A of Part Two, before
the first chapter.[16]

This has most in common with resignation, but the difference is that the conception of God is present.

An example: before God and with the conception of God, not to will to be oneself applies to what I would call a poet-existence in relation to the religious. Such a poet may have a very profound religious longing[17]. . . —*Pap.* VIII² B 161 *n.d.*, 1848

In margin of draft; see 86:31-87:5:

Offense is unhappy self-assertion over against the extraordinary, which the essentially Christian is.—*Pap.* VIII² B 164:5 *n.d.*, 1848

From draft; see 93:15-16 and 96:28-36:

N.B. It is best to remove the allusions to the dogma of hereditary sin which are found especially in chapter 2 (and anywhere else they are found). It would take me too far out, or farther than is needed here or is useful. What is appropriately stated about sin—that orthodoxy teaches that there must be a revelation to show what sin is—is not said with respect to the doctrine of hereditary sin.—*JP* V 6139 (*Pap.* VIII² B 166) *n.d.*, 1848

Deleted from final copy; see 103:5:

"In truth" (this is the way a mocker would talk, no doubt with much exaggeration; yet perhaps it would be beneficial to hear it said, even though I neither could nor would speak so falsely or mockingly), "established Christianity is an epigram on itself. That this is so becomes most clear and the epigram most biting every time one is inconsistent enough to try to do something for religion. A new holy days ordinance is put out, and it is strictly observed. Charming! If the ordinance for holy days were to be observed strictly, then first of all the churches should be closed on Sundays, for to be a pastor is indeed a livelihood and the church the pastor's shop. Why should the pastor be the only tradesman who is permitted to be open on Sunday?" Less epigrammatic than an ordinance for holy days and more in the spirit of Christianity would be to shift divine services to the weekdays and in the census to list the pastors under the rubric "Innkeepers."—*Pap.* VIII² B 171:15 *n.d.*, 1848

Deleted from final copy; see 104:20:

Is this not the sickness unto death?—*Pap.* VIII² B 171:16 *n.d.*, 1848

Deleted from final copy; see 111:20:

. . . say.*

*Note. The art of writing lines, replies, that with full tone and all imaginative intensity sound out of one passion and in which there is nevertheless the resonance of the opposite— this art no poet has practiced except the one and only: Shakespeare.—*Pap.* VIII² B 171:17 *n.d.*, 1848

See 131:35:

Drafts of: *Editor's Note*[18]
to the book "The Sickness unto Death"
—*Pap.* X⁵ B 15 *n.d.*, 1849

From draft:[19]

At the end of the book on a page by itself.   X⁵
_____   B 16
221

In closing, just this one observation with which Tertullian[20] begins his book on patience: "I confess before the Lord God that in a rather rash, perhaps even shameless way I have had the audacity to write about patience, in the practice of which I, a sinful man, am totally deficient." So also with this interpretation of ideality's demands with respect to being Christian. To my regret, I must stop there; I cannot continue and say, "So also with me"—for what similarity is there between me and Tertullian! How really audacious, virtually shameless, then, that someone ventures to interpret ideality's demands, someone who himself falls furthest short! Yet if everyone, each one individually, observed silence because no one would venture to be as shameless as that, then this unusual silence would, in fact, be another kind of shamelessness, a fraud, a cunning insurrection against God, who does not want ideality's demands to be suppressed at all. Therefore, if a better qualified person will not do it and it still has to be done, then a less qualified person must venture it and thereby involve himself in a contradiction that is, humanly speaking, a kind of treason against himself—namely, to apply himself

X⁵
B 16
222

diligently, and to concentrate totally on presenting ideality's demands, unto his own humiliation. If he succeeds, his own imperfection will show itself to be proportionately greater and greater, his shortcomings greater and greater.

That this is no platitude, a reader certainly will have no difficulty in seeing, for while he may not feel that the book applies to him, he will easily see how I must feel that it applies to me in many ways. And I am quite prepared for that; indeed, I do all I can to make myself the one who is incriminated, as if I were the only one.—*Pap.* X⁵ B 16 *n.d.*, 1849

From draft:[21]

X⁵
B 18
223
X⁵
B 18
224

Really and truly, I judge no one. Even if I myself am striving after perfection—for it would indeed be blasphemous to praise the ideal and not strive after it oneself—I nevertheless judge no one; and even if I may have a psychologist's eye—I nevertheless see people in such universality that I truly can be said to see no one—yet I judge no one.*

However, I do say—and feel obligated to do so—that I must judge myself, and not in the usual manner of speaking that is often so deceitful; and I ask the reader to interpret this in the best sense, just as it is said in that sense. Humanly speaking, the best thing about me is my author-existence. For I am personally so guilty, so very guilty, that I have been inclined to dare to regard my author-existence, its strenuous (humanly speaking) industry, its unselfishness, its reckless endeavors in the service of truth, as a slight indemnity for my personal guilt. But this author-existence of mine, regardless of any other fault it may have, has one fundamental defect: I have had independent means.[22] From an ethical point of view, this advantage is a minus that subtracts a whole quality, so that not even my author-existence is a truly ethical existence, to say nothing of a truly Christian existence in the strictest sense. To live suffering for the idea and to carry the full load of universally human responsibilities, to go on living for the idea in economic insecurity, to be married, to endure with sadness of soul the world's opposition to the idea—that is a truly ethical existence.** Every advantage subtracts, and an advantage as decisive as mine subtracts a whole quality even from the definition of truly ethical existence.

So far do I fall short. But for this very reason my portrayal of what is infinitely higher than my existence may well be authentic, but it could not possibly be authentic if I were unwilling to make this admission.[23]

*However, the book judges me in very many ways, among them because, while I may not be a poet, my existence (only that I am aware of this) is still essentially a poet-existence by my having been exempted from working for a living; I myself am the only one dealt with negatively and personally in the book.

**And this purely ethical existence is still only provisional, is different by a whole quality from the, in the strictest sense, truly Christian existence, which, humble before God, realizes that all this effort and suffering is nothing before God and yet does not quit, which furthermore (despite all its sorrow and anxieties) has essentially only one sorrow—sorrow for its sins —and essentially only one solace: the solace of the Atonement.—*Pap.* X⁵ B 18 *n.d.*, 1849

X⁵
B 18
225

From draft:

At the end on a page by itself.

Editor's Note[24]

X⁵
B 19
225

Just as, seen from the inside, it could seem not unlike an act of treason against oneself, so it could outwardly seem "rash and almost shameless" (to use a phrase that certainly does not make it better but all the worse for me, a phrase of Tertullian's and about himself, but in a similar situation) for someone to venture to interpret the demands of ideality with respect to being a Christian, someone who in any case, yet indeed in some way and perhaps in many ways, is imperfect. Yet if everyone, each one individually, observed silence because no one wanted to venture to be that traitorous, that rash, or that shameless, then this universal silence would in fact be another kind of insolence, a fraud, a cunning insurrection against God, who by no means wants ideality's demands to be suppressed.

Thus someone has ventured it, someone who is no one; I have only ventured what for me is already very audacious—to publish this presentation.

X⁵
B 19
226

Someone who is no one cannot possibly offend anyone, cannot possibly judge anyone. And if it is possible that the author does not judge anyone, in a way I myself am most concerned that that will not happen, for if he does judge someone, it will be me first and foremost. That this is no platitude, a reader certainly will have no difficulty in seeing, for although he may not feel that the book applies to him, he will easily see how I must feel that it applies to me in many ways.

It does indeed seem as if the book were written by a physician. But he who is the physician is someone who is no one; he does not say to any single human being: You are sick. Nor does he say it to me; he merely describes the sickness while he at the same time continually defines what "faith" is, which he seems to think he himself possesses to an extraordinary degree, and this presumably accounts for his name: Anti-Climacus.

On the other hand, I do all I can so that I might be the one he means—as if I were the one, the sick person, of whom he speaks—by at least striving to be one who honestly strives. And this honest effort requires first and foremost that a person be honest about ideality's demands, that he not ask that the price be lowered one jot, but willingly—yes, even more, happily, yes, even more, blissfully—finds himself in this humiliation when the ideality in reverse, or turned against me, presses down in proportion as the demand becomes greater and greater, that is, more and more true—for how could it be with ideality as it is with only the finite, that it can be enlarged falsely, that is, exaggerated. Only when ideality's demand has infinitely become as great as possible, only then is it completely true. Alas, it is only a new expression for the indigenous imperfection: to feel oneself deeply, deeply pressed down when ideality's demand is presented only somewhat truly, and then, with respect to the one presenting it, to have to doubt whether it is even possible for a person to present ideality's demand as infinite as it is!—*Pap.* X⁵ B 19 *n.d.*, 1849

From draft: [25]

. . . It does indeed seem as if the book were written by a physician, and as if Johannes Climacus, with whom the author otherwise has considerable in common, places himself so low that he even claims that he is not a Christian. [26] Thus one seems able to detect in Anti-Climacus that he thinks he himself is a Christian to an exceptional degree, also at times that Christianity is really only for geniuses, yet not defining this word with an accent on intellectuality. . . .—*Pap.* X⁵ B 20 *n.d.*, 1849

[*In margin*: About a postscript to *The Sickness unto Death.*]

At first I thought of a postscript [note] by the editor. But for one thing it is plain to see that I personally am a part of the book—for example, the part about the religious poet;[27] for another, I am afraid I thereby will contradict the argument in another book (in one of those which make up "Practice in Christianity")[28] about making observations instead of preaching.

[*In margin*: Such a postscript is completely inappropriate to the tone of the book, and in the long run humility of that sort might rather almost embitter.]

In any case, the sketches for this postscript[29] are in my desk.—*JP* VI 6437 (*Pap.* X^1 A 525) *n.d.*, 1849

About "The Sickness unto Death"

Perhaps there ought to have been, as first intended, a little postscript by the editor, for example:

Editor's Postscript [Note]

This book seems to be written by a physician; I, the editor, am not the physician, I am one of the sick.

As mentioned, it was contemplated; in fact, in my desk, there are several drafts[30] of such a postscript [note] from that time, but the fact is that at the time I did not as yet have as deep an understanding as I do now of the significance of the new pseudonym. Furthermore (as is also noted in the journal [*i.e., Pap.* X^1 A 422] from the time *The Sickness unto Death* was printed), I feared that it would be misinterpreted in various ways, as if I myself were afraid and wanted to keep myself on the outside and so on.

Now I understand perfectly that an editor's preface must always accompany the new pseudonym, Anti-Climacus, in which I say: I am striving.

There must be some kind of judgment in Christendom— *aber*, in such a way that I myself am judged. [*In margin*: see p. 50 in this journal (*i.e., Pap.* X^2 A 199).]

This is, it may be said, a kind of heroism corresponding to my nature, a synthesis of rigorousness and gentleness.—*JP* VI 6535 (*Pap.* X^2 A 204) *n.d.*, 1849

See Historical Introduction, p. xxiii:

"Let not the heart in sorrow sin"

Under this title I would like to write a few discourses dealing with the most beautiful and noble, humanly speaking, forms of despair: unhappy love, grief over the death of a beloved, sorrow at not having achieved one's proper place in the world, the forms the "poet" loves and that only Christianity dares to call sin, while the human attitude is that the lives of such people are infinitely more worthwhile than the millions that make up the prosy-pack.—*JP* VI 6277 (*Pap*. IX A 421) *n.d.*, 1848

See Historical Introduction, p. xxiii:

"Let not the heart in sorrow sin"
7 Discourses

Here the finest, the, humanly speaking, most lovable forms of despair (which is the "poets'" ultimate) are to be treated—for example, unhappy love, grief over one who is dead, grief over not having achieved one's destiny in life.

Perhaps the 3 or 4 themes left over from "States of Mind in the Strife of Suffering," which are someplace in a journal [*Pap*. VIII¹ A 500], could be combined with these. Each discourse would first of all develop or describe the particular sorrow that it is to treat; then the admonition: Let not the heart in sorrow sin—consider this: and now the theme. For example, about one who is dead—description—let not the heart in sorrow sin—consider this: the joy of it that *at last* and *for a little while* are identical (but this is used lyrically in another piece, "From on High He Will Draw All to Himself"); or consider this: the joy of it that it is for joy that one does not believe the highest etc.

But perhaps (instead of leading backward by means of joyful thoughts) it would be better to concentrate attention constantly on the infinite distinction between sorrow and sin, after having shown explicitly in each discourse how this sorrow is sin, or can become that by a hair's breadth.—*JP* VI 6278 (*Pap*. IX A 498) *n.d.*, 1848

Addition to Pap. IX A 498; *see Historical Introduction, p. xxiii:*

Let Not the Heart in Sorrow Sin
[*Changed from*: Sorrow in Sin.]

Introduction

My Listener, do you almost shudder at these words, are you seized by the anxiety that of all sins this sin might be the most dreadful. You find it almost superfluous, you look around involuntarily to see if there could be someone like this, you think of the people you have learned to know, whether among them there could be anyone like this who hides this very sin in his conscience.

If you do, you make a mistake. There is perhaps no sin as common as this one, which the old poet has described in such a way and so excellently that he did not need to say more to be remembered; no doubt there is scarcely a man who has not once in his life (if not all his life) sinned in this way, in the time of sorrow—and indeed every man has sorrow in this life. But not only this; this sin is also so well regarded among men that it is even praised and extolled. Ask "the poet" what it is that especially inspires him to songs which praise heroes and heroines—it is this very sin of the heart in sorrow. It is in fact the highest form of despair. When Juliet kills herself, or Brutus, or, if it does not go so far, when a man's mood is such that every one of his words betrays that he believes that for him and his pain, his sorrow, there is no cure either in heaven or on earth, neither from God nor with men, neither in time nor eternity—well, that is precisely when the poet becomes inspired, and it is precisely then that he has let the heart sin in sorrow.—*JP* VI 6279 (*Pap.* IX A 499) *n.d.*, 1848

Addition to Pap. IX A 498; *see Historical Introduction, p. xxiii:*

Let Not the Heart in Sorrow Sin
7 Discourses

No. 1   Let not the heart in sorrow sin   so
you abandon faith *in* God

No. 2 Let not the heart in sorrow sin   so
      you abandon faith *in men*

No. 3 Let not the heart in sorrow sin   so
      you abandon the hope *of eternity*

No. 4 Let not the heart in sorrow sin   so
      you abandon hope *for this life*

No. 5 Let not the heart in sorrow sin   so
      you abandon love *to God*

No. 6 Let not the heart in sorrow sin   so
      you abandon love *to men*

No. 7 Let not the heart in sorrow sin   so
      you abandon love *to yourself*
        —*JP* VI 6280 (*Pap.* IX A 500) *n.d.*, 1848

EDITORIAL APPENDIX

ACKNOWLEDGMENTS

The present volume is included in a general grant from the National Endowment for the Humanities. The grant includes a gift from the Danish Ministry of Cultural Affairs. A grant for special research expenses has been received from the A. P. Møller og Hustru Chastine McKinney Møllers Fond.

The translators-editors are indebted to the late Gregor Malantschuk and to Grethe Kjær for their knowledgeable observations on crucial concepts and terminology.

Robert L. Perkins, Niels Thulstrup, John Elrod, and Per Lønning, members of the international Advisory Board for *Kierkegaard's Writings*, have given helpful criticism of the manuscript on the whole and in detail.

Acknowledgment is made to Gyldendals Forlag for permission to make scholarly use of the notes to *Søren Kierkegaards Samlede Værker*.

The book collection and the microfilm collection of the Kierkegaard Library, St. Olaf College, have been used in the preparation of the text, Supplement, and Editorial Appendix.

The manuscript was typed by Dorothy Bolton, checked by John Hendricks, Michael Daugherty, Jack and Pamela Schwandt, and Steven Knudson, and guided through the press by Sanford G. Thatcher and Gretchen Oberfranc.

COLLATION OF *THE SICKNESS UNTO DEATH*
IN THE DANISH EDITIONS OF
KIERKEGAARD'S COLLECTED WORKS

Vol. XI *Ed. 1*	*Vol. XI* *Ed. 2*	*Vol. 15* *Ed. 3*	*Vol. XI* *Ed. 1*	*Vol. XI* *Ed. 2*	*Vol. 15* *Ed. 3*
114	132	66	154	173	98
117	133	67	155	174	99
118	133	68	156	175	99
121	137	69	157	176	100
122	137	69	158	178	101
123	138	70	159	179	102
127	143	73	160	180	103
128	144	73	161	181	104
129	145	74	162	183	106
130	146	75	163	184	106
131	147	76	164	185	107
132	148	77	165	186	108
133	149	78	166	187	109
134	150	79	167	188	110
135	151	80	168	189	111
136	153	81	169	191	112
137	154	81	170	192	113
138	155	82	171	193	114
139	156	84	172	194	115
140	157	85	173	195	116
141	159	86	174	196	117
142	160	87	175	197	118
143	161	87	176	198	119
144	162	88	177	200	120
145	163	89	178	201	121
146	164	90	179	202	122
147	165	91	180	203	123
148	166	92	181	204	124
149	167	93	182	206	125
150	168	94	183	207	126
151	170	95	184	208	127
152	171	96	185	209	128
153	172	97	189	213	131

Vol. XI Ed. 1	Vol. XI Ed. 2	Vol. 15 Ed. 3	Vol. XI Ed. 1	Vol. XI Ed. 2	Vol. 15 Ed. 3
190	214	131	216	243	156
191	215	132	217	245	157
192	216	133	218	246	158
193	217	134	219	247	159
194	218	135	220	248	160
195	219	136	221	249	161
196	220	137	222	250	162
197	222	138	223	252	163
198	223	139	224	253	164
199	224	140	225	254	165
200	225	141	226	255	166
201	226	142	227	256	167
202	227	143	228	257	168
203	228	144	229	258	169
204	230	145	230	259	169
205	231	146	231	260	170
206	232	147	232	261	171
207	233	148	233	262	172
208	234	149	234	264	173
209	235	150	235	265	174
210	237	151	236	266	175
211	238	152	237	267	176
212	239	153	238	268	177
213	240	154	239	269	178
214	241	155	240	270	179
215	243	156	241	271	179

NOTES

TITLE PAGE. See Supplement, p. 139 (*Pap.* VIII² B 140, 171:1-5), for alterations of the title page in the provisional draft and in the printing manuscript.

The term "psychological," which is used as a replacement for "upbuilding" (see Supplement, p. 139; *Pap.* VIII² B 140, 171:1-5), is also found in the subtitle of *The Concept of Anxiety*. Kierkegaard's conception of psychology can scarcely be equated with behavioral psychology. In the present work, the term means not primarily a description of typical psychical states but a philosophical anthropology and a phenomenology of human possibilities.

For Upbuilding and Awakening. See Historical Introduction, p. xxii and note 61; *JP* V 5686 and note 1028; VI 6438 (*Pap.* IV B 159:6; X¹ A 529). On the translation of *Opbyggelse*, see *JP* IV, p. 761.

Anti-Climacus. For entries on this late pseudonym and its relation to Kierkegaard and to Johannes Climacus, see Historical Introduction, p. xxii; *JP* VII, p. 6, Anti-Climacus, especially *JP* VI 6433 (*Pap.* X¹ A 517); *Letters*, Letters 213, 219, *KW* XXV.

Edited by S. Kierkegaard. See Historical Introduction, p. xxiii.

EPIGRAPH. See Supplement, p. 140 (*Pap.* VIII² B 171:6).

1. A free version of Romans 8:28. See also I Corinthians 14:26.
2. See *JP* IV 3854-71.
3. The expressions "the idea of man in the abstract" and "world history" are no doubt references to Hegel's philosophy, particularly to his *Phänomenologie des Geistes* and *Die Philosophie der Geschichte*. The Preface to the *Phenomenology* closes with the following paragraph:

> For the rest, at a time when the universal nature of spiritual life has become so very much emphasized and strengthened, and the mere individual aspect has become, as it should be, correspondingly a matter of indifference, when, too, that universal aspect holds, by the entire range of its substance, the full measure of the wealth it has built up, and lays claim to it all, the share in the total work of mind that falls to the activity of any particular individual can only be very small. Because this is so, the individual must all the more forget himself, as in fact the very nature of science implies and requires that he should; and he must, moreover, become and do what he

can. But all the less must be demanded of him, just as he can expect the less from himself, and may ask the less for himself.

Georg Wilhelm Friedrich Hegel's Werke. Vollständige Ausgabe, I-XVIII, ed. Ph. Marheineke et al. (Berlin: 1832-45; *ASKB* 549-65), II, p. 58; *Jubiläumsausgabe* [*J.A.*], I-XXVI (Stuttgart: 1927-40), II, p. 66; *The Phenomenology of Mind*, tr. J. B. Baillie (New York, Harper, 1967), p. 130.

The Preface to *The Philosophy of History* contains the well-known statement about world history: "But these instances of providential design are of a limited kind, and concern nothing more than the desires of the individual in question. But in the history of the World, the *Individuals* we have to do with are *Peoples*; Totalities that are States. We cannot, therefore, be satisfied with what we may call this "peddling" view of Providence, to which the belief alluded to limits itself" (*Die Philosophie der Geschichte, Werke*, IX, p. 18; *J.A.*, XI, p. 40; *The Philosophy of History*, tr. J. Sibree [New York: Collier, 1902], p. 14).

The "wonder game," also called the "wonder stool," is a game in which one person sits on a stool in the middle of a circle while another goes around quietly asking others what they wonder about the person who is "it." Upon being told what others had wondered about him, he tries to guess the source in each instance.

4. See Supplement, p. 140 (*Pap.* X¹ A 530).

5. For a concluding prayer not used, see Supplement, p. 141 (*Pap.* VIII² B 143).

6. References to Lazarus appear also in *Eighteen Upbuilding Discourses, KW* V (*SV* V 113); *Upbuilding Discourses in Various Spirits, KW* XV (*SV* VIII 259); *Works of Love, KW* XVI (*SV* IX 98, 308); *Christian Discourses, KW* XVII (*SV* X 108).

PART ONE

1. For altered portions of the final draft of this compact section, see Supplement, pp. 141-42 (*Pap.* VIII² B 170:1-2).

2. On the conception of man as a synthesis of the temporal and the eternal, see, for example, *The Concept of Irony, KW* II (*SV* XIII 163); *Either/Or*, II, *KW* IV (*SV* II 38); *The Concept of Anxiety, KW* VIII (*SV* IV 315, 319-20, 323, 328, 331, 334-35, 338, 341, 349-50, 355, 358, 360-62, 385, 390, 408, 421); *Stages, KW* XI (*SV* VI 97, 103, 106, 118, 151, 290, 382); *Postscript, KW* XII (*SV* VII 42-43, 63, 73); *The Point of View, KW* XXII (*SV* XIII 567); *JP* I 55; VI 5792 (*Pap.* VI A 102, B 18).

3. See "the first self," *Eighteen Upbuilding Discourses, KW* V (*SV* V 95-96).

4. See "the deeper self," ibid. (*SV* V 95-99).

5. See *The Concept of Anxiety, KW* VIII (*SV* IV 331, 464); *Three Discourses at the Communion on Fridays, KW* XVIII (*SV* XI 266). See Historical Introduction, p. xii; Supplement, pp. 144-47 (*Pap.* VIII² B 168:6).

6. An individual as a psycho-somatic duality is "in himself"; in relating

itself to itself, the duality is "for itself." See pp. 13-14. Cf. Sartre's *en soi* and *pour soi*. Jean-Paul Sartre, *Being and Nothingness*, tr. Hazel E. Barnes (New York: Philosophical Library, 1956), pp. 73-220, 617-28.

7. For the version of this heading in the final draft, with its emphasis upon responsibility, see Supplement, p. 142 (*Pap*. VIII² B 170:3).

8. For the longer draft version of this sentence see Supplement, p. 143 (*Pap*. VIII² B 168:2), which represents a very important complement to later lines on the qualitative difference between God and man (pp. 99, 117, 121, 126, and 127).

9. See *JP* IV 4030 (*Pap*. X² A 436).

10. See *Fragments, KW* VII (*SV* IV 237).

11. See Supplement, p. 143 (*Pap*. VIII² B 168:3).

12. See Supplement, p. 143 (*Pap*. VIII² B 170:4).

13. With reference to the remainder of the sentence and the first sentence in the next paragraph, see Supplement, pp. 143-44 (*Pap*. VIII² B 168:5).

14. With reference to the following paragraph, see Supplement, p. 144 (*Pap*. VIII² B 170:5).

15. See p. 14 and note 5 above.

16. For deleted versions of the portion prior to section c, see Supplement, pp. 144-48 (VIII² B 168:6, 170:6).

17. For the deleted portion from the opening of section c, see Supplement, p. 148 (VIII² B 170:7). See note 5 above.

18. See Supplement, p. 148 (*Pap*. VIII² B 145:3).

19. See Mark 9:48.

20. *Aut Caesar aut nihil*, the motto of Caesar Borgia. See *Stages, KW* XI (*SV* VI 144).

21. See Supplement, pp. 148-49 (*Pap*. VIII² B 168:8).

22. Plato, *Republic*, X, 608 c-610; *Platonis quae extant opera*, I-IX, ed. F. Astius (Leipzig: 1819-32; *ASKB* 1144-54), V, pp. 79-85.

23. See Supplement, p. 149 (*Pap*. VIII² B 148:4).

24. See Supplement, p. 149 (*Pap*. VIII² B 148:6).

25. See pp. 57, 100-01, 107; *JP* III 3567 (*Pap*. X¹ A 679).

26. On derivation and freedom, see *JP* II 1251 (*Pap*. VII¹ A 181).

27. On the significance of speaking, see, for example, *Fear and Trembling, KW* VI (*SV* III 155, 160-64).

28. See J. G. Fichte, *Grundriss des Eigenthümlichen der Wissenschaftslehre, Sämmtliche Werke*, I-XI (Berlin, Bonn: 1834-46; *ASKB* 489-99), I, 1, pp. 386-87. Fichte regarded the "productive power of the imagination" as the source of the concept of the external world (the *Not-I*) and of the basic categories of thought.

See Anti-Climacus, *Practice in Christianity, KW* XX (*SV* XII 173-78), where *Indbildningskraft* (also "imagination" in English) is used to stress the relation of the ethical and imagination, "the capacity for perfecting (idealizing)" (p. 178).

29. Each of the sixty members had a horn fashioned for a particular note, which was played only at appropriate times.

30. With reference to the remainder of the paragraph, see Supplement, p. 149 (*Pap.* VIII² B 150:6).

31. See Luke 10:42.

32. See Matthew 16:26.

33. With reference to the remainder of the paragraph, see Supplement, p. 150 (*Pap.* VIII² B 150:7).

34. See, for example, Plato, *Philebus*, 30 a; *Platonis opera*, III, p. 316.

35. See *Fragments, KW* VII (*SV* IV 237), and *Postscript, KW* XII (*SV* VII 296). "Necessity has been defined, and rightly so, as the union of possibility and actuality" (Hegel, *Encyclopädie der philosophischen Wissenschaften, Erster Theil, Die Logik, Werke*, VI, para. 147, p. 292; *J.A.*, VIII, p. 330; *Hegel's Logic*, tr. William Wallace [Oxford: Clarendon Press, 1975], p. 208).

36. See Supplement, p. 150 (*Pap.* VIII² B 150:8).

37. See Matthew 19:26; Mark 10:27, 14:36; Luke 1:37.

38. With reference to the remainder of the sentence, see Supplement, p. 150 (*Pap.* VIII² B 150:9). Kierkegaard quotes from *Shakespeare's dramatische Werke*, I-XII, tr. A. W. Schlegel and L. Tieck (in which II, 4 is III, 1, and therefore III, 2 is III, 3) (Berlin: 1839-40; *ASKB* 1883-88), I, p. 153.

39. See note 37 above.

40. King Midas. See Ovid, *Metamorphoses*, XI, 85-145; *Ovid Metamorphoses*, I-II, tr. F. J. Miller (Loeb, New York: Putnam, 1916), II, pp. 127-31.

41. See Supplement, p. 150 (*Pap.* VIII² 171:10).

42. See Supplement, p. 150 (*Pap.* VIII² B 171:12).

43. See Supplement, p. 150 (*Pap.* VIII² B 150:11).

44. Freely quoted from Benedict de Spinoza, *Ethics*, II, *Scholium* to *Propositio* 43; *Opera philosophica omnia*, ed. A. Gfroerer (Stuttgart: 1830; *ASKB* 788), p. 331. See *Fragments, KW* VII (*SV* VII 217); *Prefaces, KW* IX (*SV* V 62).

45. See Diogenes Laertius, II, 5, 31; *Diogenes Laertii De vitis philosophorum* (Leipzig: 1833; *ASKB* 1109), p. 75; *Diogen Laërtses filosofiske Historie*, I-II, tr. Børge Riisbrigh (Copenhagen: 1812; *ASKB* 1110-11), I, p. 70; *Stages, KW* XI (*SV* VI 295); *Postscript, KW* XII (*SV* VII 334); *Two Ages*, p. 10, *KW* XIV (*SV* VIII 10); *JP* IV 4267 (*Pap*. VII¹ A 193).

46. The paragraph is a token of Kierkegaard's polemic against Hegelianism and other system building that dissolves the individual into the whole and is thereby indifferent to individual existence, that of the thinker himself and of others. See, for example, *Fragments, KW* VII (*SV* IV 175-77, 180-81); *Postscript, KW* XII (*SV* VII 4-6, 68-73, 86-97, 101-03, 115-36, 157-61, 303-06); on Socrates, *JP* IV 4267 (*Pap.* VII¹ A 193).

47. See "The Anxiety of Spiritlessness," *The Concept of Anxiety, KW* VIII (*SV* IV 315, 363-66).

48. See *Irische Elfenmärchen* (T. C. Croker, *Fairy Legends and Traditions of the South of Ireland*, I-III [London: 1825-28]), tr. Jakob and Wilhelm Grimm (Leipzig: 1826; *ASKB* 1423), p. lxxxiii.

49. Cf. Augustine, *The City of God*, XIX, 25; *Sancti Aurelii Augustini . . . opera*, I-XVII (Bassani: 1797-1807; *ASKB* 117-34), Vol. IX, pp. 750-51; *Fragments, KW* VII (*SV* IV 219-20).

50. This view of suicide holds for the Stoics but not, for example, for Socrates and Plato. See *Phaedo*, 61-62.

51. Anachronism.

52. See *The Concept of Anxiety, KW* VIII (*SV* IV 365).

53. See Supplement, p. 151 (*Pap.* VIII² B 171:13). Presumably the deleted (D) refers to a contemplated section that was never written. The question of despair in relation to self-knowledge is touched upon in the footnote on pp. 60-61. See Supplement, p. 153 (*Pap.* VIII² B 156).

54. For draft forms of the following paragraph, see Supplement, p. 151 (*Pap.* VIII² B 151, 152, 153:1).

55. With reference to the remainder of this sentence, see Supplement, p. 152 (*Pap.* VIII² B 153:3).

56. For marginal additions to the draft version of the preceding part of this paragraph, see Supplement, p. 152 (*Pap.* VIII² B 154:3).

57. See, for example, *Postscript, KW* XII (*SV* VII 37-38); *JP* I 372, 407 (*Pap.* VIII¹ A 392; XI¹ A 503).

58. Goethe, *Faust*, Part I, Sc. IV (Mephistopheles); *Goethe's Werke*, I-LV (Stuttgart, Tübingen: 1828-33, *ASKB* 1641-48), XII, p. 91.

59. "We Trojans, with Ilium and all its Teucrian glory, / Are things of the past" (Virgil, *Aeneid*, II, 325; *The Aeneid of Virgil*, I-II, tr. C. Day Lewis, [London: Hogarth Press, 1954], I, p. 40).

60. In the Danish there is a play on the two expressions: *at hele* (to heal) and *Hæler*.

61. With reference to the heading and to the next two paragraphs, see Supplement, pp. 152-53 (*Pap.* VIII² B 155).

62. See p. 47 and note 53. For a draft version of the remainder of this footnote, see Supplement, p. 153 (*Pap.* VIII² B 156).

63. See *The Point of View, KW* XXII (*SV* XIII 546).

64. With reference to the remainder of the paragraph, see Supplement, p. 153 (*Pap.* VIII² B 157:3).

65. *Richard the Third*, IV, 4; *Shakespeare's Werke*, tr. Schlegel and Tieck, III, p. 339. See Supplement, p. 154 (*Pap.* VIII² B 157:5).

66. With reference to the preceding paragraph, see Supplement, pp. 154-55 (*Pap.* VIII² B 158), first paragraph.

67. Genesis 1:1.

68. See Matthew 16:19.

69. See *Either/Or*, II, *KW* IV (*SV* II 145).

70. See *The Point of View, KW* XXII (*SV* XIII 560, 569, 571).

71. See Supplement, p. 155 (*Pap.* VIII² B 159:4).

72. Probably a reference to the third legend in the story of Rübezahl. I. A. Musäus, *Volksmärchen der Deutschen,* I-V (Gotha: 1826), II, pp. 62-63; *Musæus Folkeæventyr*, I-III, tr. F. Schaldemose (Copenhagen: 1840), II, pp. 65-66. Presumably Kierkegaard knew one or both of these, but they are not listed in *ASKB*.

73. See pp. 50-60.

PART TWO

1. See Supplement, pp. 155-56 (*Pap.* VIII² B 161).

2. With reference to the following passage on poet-existence, see Supplement, pp. 154-55 (*Pap.* VIII² B 158), paragraph two; see also *The Lily of the Field and the Bird of the Air* (1849), *KW* XVIII (*SV* XI 11-13, 21).

3. See *Three Discourses at the Communion on Fridays* (1849), *KW* XVIII (*SV* XI 254-55).

4. See *Postscript*, *KW* XII (*SV* VII 462-63); *Three Discourses at the Communion on Fridays* (1849), *KW* XVIII (*SV* XI 265-67).

5. On the term "reality" (*Realitet*), see *JP* III, pp. 900-03.

6. See, for example, *Augsburg Confession*, Articles II and IV.

7. Dogmatics influenced primarily by Kant, who in *The Critique of Practical Reason* maintained that moral law is derived from man's rational consciousness, man's rational legislating capacity, and that man does not need the conception of God to be able to recognize his duty.

8. See Ephesians 2:12.

9. See *The Concept of Anxiety*, *KW* VIII (*SV* IV 300).

10. See p. 46 and note 49.

11. See *JP* VI 6689 (*Pap.* X³ A 551).

12. See Luke 11:15 and 26.

13. Kierkegaard's various writings are in a number of forms, for example, the lyrical effusions of "Diapsalmata" in *Either/Or*, I, the "dialectical lyric" (subtitle of *Fear and Trembling*), and the "algebraic" form (so designated in the works themselves) of *The Concept of Anxiety*, *KW* VIII (*SV* IV 382, 395, 403), *Philosophical Fragments*, *KW* VII (*SV* IV 254), and *The Sickness unto Death*. The term refers to the compact and dialectical character of the latter works. See *JP* VI 6137 (*Pap.* VIII¹ A 652).

14. See *JP* IV 4020 (*Pap.* X¹ A 384).

15. On these crucial themes, see *JP* I 5-12; III 3025-40, 3070-3102.

16. See pp. 127-28 and notes; *Practice in Christianity*, *KW* XX (*SV* XII 67-134).

17. See I Corinthians 2:9. See p. 118; *Fragments*, *KW* VII (*SV* IV 178, 203).

18. The Danish term *Kjøbstad* (market town) is a play on the name Copenhagen (*Kjøbenhavn*), which literally means "market harbor." See *The Point of View*, *KW* XXII (*SV* XIII 580-82), where Kierkegaard writes of his fate of being a "genius in a market town." In 1845 the population of Copenhagen was 126,787.

19. See, for example, *Two Ages*, pp. 81-96, *KW* XIV (*SV* VIII 76-89).

20. See Supplement, p. 156 (*Pap.* VIII² B 164:5).

21. See Aristotle, *Nicomachean Ethics*, 1108 c-1109 c. Kierkegaard owned twenty-two sets and single works of Aristotle in Greek, Latin, German, and Danish (*ASKB* 1056-95). See also Horace, *Odes*, Book II, X, 5; *Q. Horatii Flacci: Opera* (Leipzig: 1828; *ASKB* 1248). For an earlier use of "plated," see *Two Ages*, p. 68, *KW* XIV (*SV* VIII 64), and note 16.

22. See Luke 22:48.

23. This is a negative formulation of the Socratic thesis that knowledge is virtue, that knowledge is possession of soul, and that it is therefore inconceivable that one knowingly does wrong. See *The Concept of Irony, KW* II (*SV* XIII 155, 234, 290).

24. This is a key term from Kant's ethics, embodying universal applicability as the main criterion of a maxim of action and presupposing that "ought" implies "can."

25. See Holberg, *Den politiske Kandestøber* (*The Political Tinker*), IV, 2; *The Point of View, KW* XXII (*SV* XIII 581).

26. Most likely a reference to Bishop J. P. Mynster.

27. See Philippians 2:7.

28. See Matthew 27:67; Luke 18:32.

29. See Mark 9:5.

30. See *Irony, KW* II (*SV* XIII 130 fn.); *On My Work as an Author, KW* XXII (*SV* XIII 508); *The Moment,* No. 2, *KW* XXIII (*SV* XIV 138); *JP* III 3540, 3689; VI 6803 (*Pap.* XI² A 281; X⁴ A 190, 557).

31. See Supplement, p. 156 (*Pap.* VIII² B 166).

32. Hegelian philosophy. See, for example, *Postscript, KW* XII (*SV* VII 119-22).

33. The indubitable halting point in Descartes's process of doubting everything dubitable. See *Meditations,* Meditation II; *The Principles of Philosophy,* Part One, I-II; *Opera philosophica Editio ultima,* I-II (Amsterdam: 1685; *ASKB* 473), I, pp. 9-14, II, pp. 2-3. See *Johannes Climacus, KW* VII (*Pap.* IV B 2:10); *Postscript, KW* XII (*SV* VII 272-73); *JP* I 1033; III 2113, 2338 (*Pap.* V A 30; II A 159; IV C 11).

34. See Matthew 8:13; *Works of Love, KW* XVI (*SV* IX 358-65).

35. See Supplement, p. 156 (*Pap.* VIII² B 166).

36. See *Fragments, KW* VII (*SV* IV 184-85).

37. See p. 95 and note 35.

38. Presumably a reference particularly to Professor H. L. Martensen, with whom Kierkegaard studied from 1837 to 1839 and whose *Den christelige Dogmatik* (*ASKB* 653) appeared in 1849.

39. See Spinoza, *Ethics,* V, 36, 40; *Opera philosophica omnia,* ed. A. Gfroerer (Stuttgart: 1830; *ASKB* 788); *Either/Or,* I, *KW* III (*SV* I 23); *Postscript, KW* XII (*SV* VII 63).

40. Psalms 111:10.

41. On the Delphic oracle's statement about Socrates, see Plato, *Apology,* 20 d-21 a; *Platonis opera,* IX, p. 27.

42. Cf. *Three Discourses at the Communion on Fridays* (1849), *KW* XVIII (*SV* XI 266-67, 274); *Practice in Christianity, KW* XX (*SV* XII 60).

43. See p. 96 and note 36.

44. See Micah 7:19.

45. See Galatians 3:22.

46. P. 96.

47. See Revelation 3:16.

48. See Mark 2:7; Luke 5:32; Romans 8:30, 9:24; I Corinthians 1:9, 7:15-24; Galatians 5:13; Ephesians 4:1-4; Colossians 3:15; I Thessalonians 2:12, 4:7,

5:24; II Thessalonians 2:14; I Timothy 6:12; II Timothy 1:9; Hebrews 2:11, 9:15; I Peter 1:15, 2:9, 21, 3:9, 5:10; II Peter 1:3. Kierkegaard does not dispute Luther's association of helpful occupations with the one common Christian calling, but he protests the reduction of the call or vocation to occupation or career and the particular form of this reduction in the specialized use of "call" for an ecclesiastical appointment. See *Upbuilding Discourses in Various Spirits*, Part One, "Purity of Heart," *KW* XV (*SV* VIII 228-37); *JP* I 227-39; IV 4946-49, 5009-15.

49. For a portion deleted from the printing manuscript, see Supplement, pp. 156-57 (*Pap.* VIII² B 171:15).

50. The term "anticlimax" has here the ordinary meaning of a decrease in the importance or impressiveness of what is said or done and is totally unrelated to the name of the pseudonymous author Anti-Climacus.

51. See Supplement, p. 157 (VIII² B 171:16).

52. Romans 14:23.

53. See Matthew 7:13; *The Point of View*, *KW* XXII (*SV* XIII 567).

54. *Shakespeare's Werke*, tr. Schlegel and Tieck, XII, p. 314. In the quotation, *Sünden* (plural) is given as *Sünde* (singular). The original English reads: "Things bad begun make strong themselves by ill."

55. See *JP* IV 4025, 4029 (*Pap.* X² A 74, 429).

56. Part One, XIV ("Forest and Cavern"), end; *Goethe's Werke*, XII, p. 176.

57. Act II, scene 3 (scene 2 in the Schlegel-Tieck translation, XII, p. 301). See *The Concept of Anxiety*, *KW* VIII (*SV* IV 412).

58. For a deletion from the printing manuscript, see p. 157 (*Pap.* VIII² B 171:17).

59. See pp. 60-61, fn.

60. See *Postscript*, *KW* XII (*SV* VII 517); *Three Discourses at the Communion on Fridays* (1849), *KW* XVIII (*SV* XI 265-69).

61. See p. 90 and note on Kant.

62. See Matthew 9:2-3; Mark 2:7.

63. The first refers to Hegel's idealism and the second to the materialism of the inverted Hegelian, Ludwig A. Feuerbach, and the assertion that in ordinary religion God is man's projection of himself. Kierkegaard owned Feuerbach's *Abälard und Heloise oder der Schriftsteller und der Mensch* (Ansbach: 1834; *ASKB* 1637); *Geschichte der neuern Philosophie* (Ansbach: 1837; *ASKB* 487); *Das Wesen des Christenthums* (2 ed., Leipzig: 1843; *ASKB* 488). See *JP* III 3477 (*Pap.* VIII¹ A 434, beginning).

64. See I Corinthians 14:33.

65. See *Politics*, III, 11, 1281 a, 40-43, and 1281 b, 15-20. If this is the portion to which Kierkegaard refers, he makes selective use of it, for Aristotle argues both sides of the mass/individual-expert issue. *JP* III 2922-3010.

66. Presumably a reference to David F. Strauss, who in his *Leben Jesu* (Berlin: 1836), II, para. 147, pp. 734 ff., maintains that the God-man is mankind.

67. A reference to political events in Denmark in 1848. See *JP* III 2933-45, IV 4131-37 VI 6310 (*Pap.* X¹ A 42).

68. See p. 84 and note 17.

69. See p. 93 and note 33.

70. See "At a Grave," the third discourse in *Three Discourses on Imagined Occasions, KW* X (*SV* V 242).

71. See Matthew 10:29.

72. The *via negationis* defines God by denying all finite and imperfect characteristics, and the *via eminentiae* by affirming in perfection all positive characteristics. See *Fragments, KW* VII (*SV* IV 212).

73. See Plato, *Apology*, 27 b; *Platonis opera*, IX, p. 43.

74. See Matthew 12:31-32; Mark 3:29; Luke 12:10.

75. In *King Henry the Fourth*, the Prince of Wales, later Henry V, is presented as a companion of Falstaff.

76. Luther's concluding reply at the Diet of Worms.

77. See Matthew 11:28; *Practice in Christianity, KW* XX (*SV* XII 5-68).

78. See Matthew 11:6; *Practice in Christianity, KW* XX (*SV* XII 69-144).

79. See Plutarch, "*De garrulitate*," 8, *Moralia*, 506 a; *Plutarch's Moralia*, I-XVII, tr. F. C. Babbitt et al. (Loeb, Cambridge: Harvard University Press, 1927-67), VI, p. 417: "in speaking we have men as teachers, but in keeping silent we have gods, and we receive from them this lesson of silence at initiations into the Mysteries." Kierkegaard owned Plutarch's *Moralia* in one Latin edition and in three German editions (*ASKB* 1172-77, 1178-80, 1190-91, 1192-96).

80. See John 10:30, 17:21.

81. See Mark 14:41.

82. See Matthew 11:5-6.

83. Paul's words in I Corinthians 11:28, preceded by his quoting of the words of institution.

84. See Matthew 26:31.

85. See I Corinthians 15:19.

86. See Luke 17:5.

87. See Luke 18:8.

88. See Heinrich Heine, "*Die Heimkehr*," *Buch der Lieder* (Hamburg: 1837), pp. 232-34; *JP* II 1730 (*Pap.* III B 16).

89. Until the new constitution of 1848, the Royal Law of 1655 was the basis of Danish law. The source of the quotation has not been located.

90. Matthew 22:42.

91. See Matthew 9:34, 12:24; Mark 3:22.

92. See Supplement, pp. 157-58 (X⁵ B 15-16, 18-20).

SUPPLEMENT

1. See *Postscript, KW* XII (*SV* VII 537-39).

2. Ibid., p. 538.

3. Ibid., p. 539.

4. See Preface, p. 6.

5. See pp. 19-20.

6. On divine omnipotence and human freedom, see the remarkable journal entry *JP* II 1251 (*Pap.* VII¹ A 181).

7. Ibid.

8. See p. 14 and note 6.

9. See note 6 above.

10. Johannes Ewald, *"En aandelig Sang,"* Samtlige Skrifter, I-IV (Copenhagen: 1780-91; *ASKB* 1533-36), I, p. 299. See *JP* IV 4731 (*Pap.* IV A 48).

11. See *Either/Or*, I, *KW* III (*SV* I 196); Hegel, *Phänomenologie des Geistes, Werke*, II, pp. 158-73; *J.A.*, II, pp. 166-81; *The Phenomenology of Mind*, tr. J. B. Baillie (2 ed., London: Allen and Unwin; New York: Macmillan, 1931), pp. 251-67.

12. See pp. 87-96.

13. See pp. 19-20.

14. See pp. 60-67.

15. Ibid.

16. See p. 79.

17. See pp. 77-78.

18. See Supplement, pp. 157-62 (*Pap.* X⁵ B 16, 18-20; X¹ A 525; X² A 204).

19. See Supplement, pp. 157-62 (*Pap.* X⁵ B 15, 18-20; X¹ A 525; X² A 204).

20. *Of Patience*, I, opening sentence; *Nyt theologisk Bibliothek*, I-XX, ed. Jens Møller (Copenhagen: 1821-32; *ASKB* 336-45), XVI, p. 64.

21. See Supplement, pp. 157-62 (*Pap.* X⁵ B 15, 16, 19, 20; X¹ A 525; X² A 204).

22. See *JP* V 6134 (*Pap.* VIII¹ A 648) and note 1796.

23. To Kierkegaard, "admission" was a crucial term and a requisite act ethically and religiously, and the absence of admission was the prime factor in his later critique of the established order. See, for example, *JP* V 6070; VI 6727 (*Pap.* VIII¹ A 388; X⁴ A 33).

24. See Supplement, pp. 157-62 (*Pap.* X⁵ B 15, 16, 18, 20; X¹ A 525; X² A 204).

25. See Supplement, pp. 157-62 (*Pap.* X⁵ B 15, 16, 18, 19; X¹ A 525; X² A 204).

26. See *Postscript*, *KW* XII (*SV* VII 537-39).

27. See pp. 77-78.

28. *Practice in Christianity*, *KW* XX (*SV* XII 213-16).

29. See Supplement, pp. 157-61 (*Pap.* X⁵ B 15, 16, 18-20).

30. Ibid.

BIBLIOGRAPHICAL NOTE

For general bibliographies of Kierkegaard studies, see:

Jens Himmelstrup, *Søren Kierkegaard International Bibliografi.* Copenhagen: Nyt Nordisk Forlag Arnold Busck, 1962.
Aage Jørgensen, *Søren Kierkegaard-litteratur 1961-1970.* Aarhus: Akademisk Boghandel, 1971.
Kierkegaard: A Collection of Critical Essays, ed. Josiah Thompson. New York: Doubleday (Anchor Books), 1972.
Søren Kierkegaard's Journals and Papers, ed. and tr. Howard V. Hong and Edna H. Hong, assisted by Gregor Malantschuk, I. Bloomington, Indiana: Indiana University Press, 1967.

For topical bibliographies of Kierkegaard studies, see ibid., I, II (1970), III-IV (1975).

INDEX

abandonment, of faith, 164; of hope, 165; of love, 165
abolition of the ethical, 114
absolute, the, 103
absorption, 111-12, 114
abstraction, 31, 90, 98, 118-19, 121-22; infinite, 55; of self, 70-72, 155; of will, 149. *See also* possibility, abstract; self, abstraction of; universality, abstract
absurd, the, 71, 83, 87
abuse of language, 51
abyss, 129; chasmic, 122
acoustics, 144, 145
act, 68; despair as, 62, 67
actuality, xvi, 34, 63, 93-94, 140; of despair, 49, 142; and logic, 97-98; necessity as unity of possibility and, 36; as negation, 15; observation of, 49; of personality, 5; and possibility, 15, 36; tension of, xix; as unity of possibility and necessity, 36
admiration and envy, 86
admiring, 86
admission, 182
adoration and offense, 86
adult, 8, 49, 58-60; despair of, 59-60
advantage, 15, 159
age, 91; of despair, ix; and hope, 38; and self-consciousness, 59
alcoholic analogy, 108
algebra, dialectical, xiv-xv
algebraic, the, xiii, 82, 178
ambiguity of Socratic definition, 88
analogy, alcoholic, 108; balloonist, 110; emperor and laborer, 84; jack, 101-02; king, 130; knot, 93; swing,

93; telegraph, 124. *See also* metaphor
Andersen, Hans Christian, *Only a Fiddler*, ix-x
anguish, 77-78. *See also* anxiety
animal and man, 15, 58, 118, 121, 143
animal category, 118. *See also* crowd, the
annihilation of possibility, 15
"anthropological contemplation," x-xi
anthropology, of despair, x; philosophical, 173
anthropomorphism, 123
"Anti," xxii
antiquity, 64
anxiety, ix, xi, xi-xiii, 44, 47, 164, 176; concept of, xi; and despair, xiii; forms of, xii-xiii; and happiness, 25; and ignorance, 44; and nothing, 25-26; and possibility, 22, 37; presupposition of, xi; about sin, 112; and the unknown, 22. *See also* anguish
appalling, the, 34
appearances, 22
approach to God, 114
Aristotle, 118; *Nicomachean Ethics*, 178; *Politics*, 180
Ast, Friedrich (Fredericus Astius), 175, 176, 179, 181
ataraxia, 69
Atonement, 100; solace of, 159
Augsburg Confession, 178
Augustine, Aurelius, *The City of God*, 176
Aut Caesar aut nihil, 175

Sartre, Jean-Paul, *Being and Nothingness*, 175
Schaldemose, Frederik Julius, 177
Schlegel, August Wilhelm, 176, 177, 180
scholarliness, 5
scienticity, 5
Scripture, 81
secret, 65
secular mentality, 33-35
self, ix, xiv, 13-14, 16, 61; abstraction of, 70-72, 155; acting, 68; actual, 20; attempt to despair, 38; becoming fantastic, 31; becoming of, 30, 35-36; before Christ, 113; coming into existence, 30; concept of, 13-14; concrete, 30, 68, 72; conscious as, 26; and consciousness, 29-30; consciousness of, 34-35, 67-68, 79, 99-100, 105; criterion of, 79-81, 114; deeper, ix, 64, 174; denial of, 99; dialectic of, 33, 35, 61, 153; dissolution of, 69-70; empirical, 56; establishment of, 20; and the eternal, 79; examination of, 128; and externalities, 55-56; finitizing of, 30-32; and finitude, 35; the first, 174; first and deeper, ix; as freedom, 29; before God, 26-27, 32, 35, 46, 77-78, 79-82, 121; ideal, 20; ignorance of, 46, 82; infinite, 68-70, 72; infinitizing of, 30-32, 34; and infinitude, 35; intended to become, 33; intensified, 100; and inwardness, 55-57; lack of, 32-35; loss of, xi, 31-36, 40-41, 61-62, 105, 110, 148-49; love to, 165; lower, 82; and necessity, 35-36, 40, 54; negative, 68, 70; "not to will to be a," 52-53; and possibility, 31, 35-36, 40; power that establishes, 14, 20, 49, 142, 144; and reflection, 31; as a relation, 13, 16, 29, 49, 144, 146-47; and relationship to God, 30; re-

sponsibility for, 55; selfish, 110; sickness of, 142; as spirit, xii, 13, 26, 46, 57, 107; as synthesis, 29-30, 35, 40, 146-47; a task, 35; theological, 79; true relation of, 147; and will, 29; will not to be, 67, 113; will to be, 67, 113; without despair, xii, 6, 14-15, 26, 30, 49, 131, 142, 147, 151; without offense, 129
self-assertion, 86; offense and unhappy, 156
self-consciousness, 26, 29-30, 34-35, 67-68, 79, 99-100, 105; and age, 59; intensification of, 113-14; levels of, 48, 71-72, 79-87, 113; and suicide, 48-49. *See also* awareness; consciousness
self-consuming, despair as, 18-21
self-destruction, xix
selfhood and equality, 27-28
self-importance, 115-16
selfishness, 110-12
self-knowledge, xii, 22-23, 31, 47-48; loss of, 53
self-love, *see* love
self-redoubling, 69
self-surrender, 86
self-willfulness, 81-82
sensate, the, 43
sensuality, 66
separation, 122
sermons, xxi
servant, form of God, 128
sewing analogy, 93
shadowboxing analogy, 69
Shakespeare, William, 150, 157; *King John*, 150; *Macbeth*, 106, 110; *Richard II*, 38, 150; *Henry IV*, 126, 181
shamelessness, 158, 160
shed metaphor, 43
Sibree, J., 174
sickness, 7-9, 16, 22, 23-28, 141; despair as, 6, 24; as dialectical qualification, 25; imaginary, 23; of self,

ADVISORY BOARD

KIERKEGAARD'S WRITINGS